HIS WORD
IN MY HEART

HIS WORD IN MY HEART

Memorizing Scripture for a Closer Walk with God

JANET POPE

MOODY PUBLISHERS

CHICAGO

All Scripture quotations, unless otherwise indicated, are taken from the Holy Bible, New International Version®, NIV®. Copyright ©1973, 1978, 1984 by Biblica, Inc.™ Used by permission of Zondervan. All rights reserved worldwide. www.zondervan.com

Scripture quotations marked NASB are taken from the *New American Standard Bible®*, Copyright © 1960, 1962, 1963, 1968, 1971, 1972, 1973, 1975, 1977, 1995 by The Lockman Foundation. Used by permission. (www.Lockman.org)

Scripture quotations marked KJV are taken from the King James Version.

Edited by Annette Laplaca
Interior design: Ragont Design
Cover design: ThinkPen Design
Cover image: © 2013 Shutterstock / 108379676

Library of Congress Cataloging-in-Publication Data

Pope, Janet.
    His word in my heart : memorizing scripture for a closer walk with God / Janet Pope.
        pages cm
    Includes bibliographical references.
    ISBN 978-0-8024-0964-5
    1. Bible—Memorizing. I. Title.
BS617.7.P66 2013
220.07—dc23
                                                    2013013126

We hope you enjoy this book from Moody Publishers. Our goal is to provide high-quality, thought-provoking books and products that connect truth to your real needs and challenges. For more information on other books and products written and produced from a biblical perspective, go to www.moodypublishers. com or write to:

Moody Publishers
820 N. LaSalle Boulevard
Chicago, IL 60610

3 5 7 9 10 8 6 4 2

Printed in the United States of America

To Ethan,
Your constancy harbors me,
your sacrifice propels me,
your assurance buoys me.

CONTENTS

INTRODUCTION

THE CHRISTIAN LIFE IS AN ODYSSEY—an unpredictable, arduous journey with many bends in the road and surprise encounters along the way. As travelers in a strange place we have no control over the elements: the cold, the wind, the darkness. Uncertainty pervades, hardships abound, and obstacles lurk in the shadows. The struggles we each face will vary, but we share a common destination. When our Father calls us home, He guarantees our arrival. The issue is not where we are going, but how we will get there.

Twenty years ago, at a fork in the road, my life took the path that led me to where I am today. The forthcoming details share the essence of my story. Inspired by an unknown woman, I began to memorize long passages and entire books of the Bible. Two small children and a never-ending list of things to do left no extra time slots in my day. I reasoned that if God wanted me to know Him and His Word, He would make a way. He wouldn't require something of me and then make it impossible to achieve.

I trained myself to use moments throughout my day to memorize Scripture when my hands were busy but my mind was free. Household chores required busyness but not thoughtfulness, so I included Scripture memory in my daily routines: showering, drying my hair, folding laundry, vacuuming, waiting in traffic or at the dentist's office. Idle minutes became opportunities to get to know God's Word.

Over the years, this practice has added up to an enormous amount of Scripture memory: 140 chapters so far. However, it's not the accomplishment that has changed my life but rather the process of thinking and meditating on specific truth learned in its context. I saw a major difference between memorizing scattered verses and memorizing verses that follow each other sequentially. I learned whole truth, not fragments, fit together the way God had intended. I experienced new depth in my relationship with God as I got to know His Word one verse at a time.

My initial motivation was strictly personal; I wanted to get closer to God for my own well-being. But I also knew how much influence a mother has on her children. Without wisdom from God, where would I lead them? God's Word, continually on my heart and mind, brought insight and discernment to each new situation. As a mother, I wanted to teach my children the way in which they should go, and now that role was less arbitrary.

Scripture memory became my platform as people called, asking me to share my story with the women of their church. Why? Because they too were desperate to have God's Word as a constant source of nourishment for their weary souls. As I travel and speak across the country, I've found that women don't want to postpone a closer walk with God until they have more time. Women hungry for God need Him today.

In this book I present an alternative for the frazzled, guilt-ridden woman who longs to know God and His Word but hasn't yet found a way to accomplish this amidst the unrelenting treadmill of activities. I cannot add one more hour to your day, but I can help you change the minutes and the moments you already have. My desire is to be intensely practical. Take my experience and my suggestions and adapt them to your own situation; find what works for you.

At a speaking engagement in Tulsa, a woman thanked me for my message. She said, "I've got to change my thinking habits. With all the bad news in our country, I find myself meditating on all the *whys* and *what-ifs*, and I'm emotionally exhausted at the end of the day. I can see that my whole outlook would change if I would meditate on God's Word instead."

I hope to lead you to the oasis of God's Word, to inspire you to trade your thoughts for God's. As you give your attention to His Word, He will meet you in unexpected places—amidst the laundry pile and the dish pile, in the carpool line and the drive-thru line. Your relationship with God will grow deeper and richer than you ever imagined. As your constant companion, He'll become an intimate confidant.

On our pilgrimage through this life unforeseen hurdles await us, but the road was never meant to be traveled alone. God gave us His Word to guide us through the lonely valleys and immovable mountains we face. For me, the journey takes on new meaning. Though night approaches, I move forward unafraid. An illuminated path shows me the way, one step at a time, with His Word in my heart.

1»
MY STORY: A NEW ROAD

AN EMPTY HOUSE, A STUFFED U-Haul, and exhaust fumes on the rise signaled the time to leave. Four-year-old Austin and six-year-old Natalie, eager to ride with their dad for the five-hundred-mile trip, left me in peaceful solitude in my own car. My week flashed back—crumpled newspapers, labeled boxes, and please-don't-leave hugs. As we ascended the ramp onto Interstate 20, leaving Dallas in my rearview mirror, I visualized God taking us in a new direction, on a new road, to a new life—in Hattiesburg, Mississippi.

After an hour of driving, the Christian radio station faded. Now alone with my thoughts, I relived memories from the last eight years: three houses remodeled while living in them (marriage still intact), hunting for antiques in those smothering barns in Forney, and hilarious moments at Supper Club. A difficult pregnancy turned to joy when a daughter arrived. Two years later, a son. Those tender years glued us together as a family, and we grew. Snapshots etched in my mind reveal a snowman and two frozen-cheeked toddlers, a blow-up swimming pool and dancing in the sprinklers. We'll always remember the Texas State Fair, Bagelsteins, the Mesquite Rodeo, and of course, America's Team and ours, the Dallas Cowboys. Friends gathered every Fourth of July for all-you-can-peel shrimp and homemade Butterfinger ice cream. Leaving Dawna, my let's-get-together friend, tugged at my resolve. Together we had trudged through newlywed confusion and newborn exhaustion. That chapter now closed.

The blessings in Texas would have made it easy to stay, but new opportunities waited for us in Mississippi. God's proven faithfulness assured me of special things ahead. Fear of the future would not rule the day. High hopes carried me to my destination.

We bought a seventy-year-old house, already remodeled by the previous owner and surrounded by trees—big, tall trees. We made new friends, joined a dynamic church, and got busy with life.

A year went by. Nothing terrible happened, but a growing sense of disappointment loomed over me. It was not a mid-life crisis at thirty-five, but rather unfulfilled expectations. I was not where I wanted to be in my life. I made known to God my frustration and waited for His reply.

About that time, four new friends invited me to go with them to a Christian conference at Precept Ministries in Chattanooga, Tennessee, six hours away. If nothing else, I needed a break from the Mom routine, and I knew I would enjoy the fellowship. It's strange to me now that I look back on this conference as a turning point in my life.

One morning, while singing songs, the worship leader saw someone she knew in the audience and called her to the front spontaneously. With giddy enthusiasm the song leader asked her friend to share some Scripture with this group of about 300. Without hesitation, this unnamed woman recited from memory the entire book of Colossians. Awe-inspiring! I sat in my chair mesmerized by what I had just heard. The wheels turned in my mind. I wondered what it would be like to really know God's Word, to have it so embedded in my heart and mind that I would carry it with me wherever I would go. What would it mean to my relationship with God if I really knew His Word?

I had become a Christian at twenty-one years old, while a student at the University of Florida. But I didn't grow up in church and had no Bible background or knowledge accumulated. In the years that followed, I read through the Bible many times. In fact, I held to a daily Bible-reading regimen. But I couldn't confidently say that I knew the Bible. My Bible knowledge resembled a tangled pile of disconnected wires.

I came home from the conference in Chattanooga determined to make a change. I had come face-to-face with the shallowness of my own Bible knowledge, and I longed to go deeper. But where would I begin? Since my inspiration had come from someone who memorized Scripture, I decided to follow her lead. I started with the book of Ephesians, an impossible undertaking without God's help. It took me several months, but I worked on it every single day and night, learning one verse at a time.

My overriding motivation was the fear of quitting. At this point in my life, I couldn't handle the devastation of another goal abandoned. The day came when I shared, from memory, the book of Ephesians with my Sunday school class. As I concluded with "Grace to all who love our Lord Jesus Christ with an undying love," tears flowed and my heart pounded with joy. I saw others with tears in their eyes as well, but I didn't understand what it all meant. That day I reached a milestone in my life; the stepping-stones that preceded it were the months I spent devouring Ephesians chapter by chapter.

I couldn't say that I knew God's Word yet. What I could say was, "I know the book of Ephesians." And for the first time in my Christian life, I felt as though God's Word was knowable. I had proven that to myself. For years I'd viewed knowing the Bible as something unattainable, or perhaps reserved for a select few. Now I was convinced that the knowledge of the Bible was not beyond my reach.

At the same time, I saw the inexhaustible nature of God's Word. Even within the book of Ephesians, after memorizing every single word, more discoveries awaited me. I had not yet reached the depth of its truth.

Another outcome grew out of many months spent in Ephesians—a sense of ownership, as if God had written the book just for me. Every time I heard anything from Ephesians mentioned, in conversation or at church, I immediately thought, *That's my book.* I had poured hours of my life into Ephesians, and it now belonged to me.

But why did God give me His Word, and where did He want to take me from there? I didn't know. I felt as if I were at a crossroad in my life. I couldn't go back, and I couldn't stay the same; those options seemed closed. I wasn't sure why or what was ahead, but I saw myself standing at a crossroad, calculating a move to the right or to the left.

On my upcoming fall schedule I planned to teach a Bible study on 2 Peter. Because it was several months away, I decided to memorize that book. With only three chapters I could do it over the summer. As I began in chapter 1, saying the words over and over, I noticed a theme unfolding.

> Grace and peace be yours in abundance *through the knowledge of God* and of Jesus our Lord. (2 Peter 1:2, emphasis added)
>
> His divine power has given us everything we need

for life and godliness *through our knowledge of him* who called us by his own glory and goodness. (2 Peter 1:3, emphasis added)

Through these he has given us *his very great and precious promises* so that through them you may participate in the divine nature . . . (2 Peter 1:4, emphasis added)

I meditated not only on the words but on the truth presented there. And I began to have a conversation with myself that went something like this: *Wow! These are very bold statements. How could they possibly be true?* This passage claims that through our knowledge of God

- we can have grace and peace in abundance,
- we can have everything we need for life and godliness, and
- we can participate in the divine nature; we can become more like Jesus.

Is this possible? I asked. Of course, I know God's Word is true "in theory," but if it is really true that we can have everything we need for life and godliness, through our knowledge of God, then how come more Christians aren't pouring themselves into the Scriptures so they can have all these things? I don't know! Then I asked myself, *Well, how come you don't?* I sat there contemplating my own challenge. Then I determined, *I'm going to! I am going to pour myself into God's Word until I get everything I need for life and godliness.*

That day I made the right turn at the crossroad. With renewed fervor, I plunged into God's Word as though there were no tomorrow—every free minute of every day and night. As a busy mom with no extra hours in my day, I had to find ways to fit in God's Word. I agonized while determining which activities were truly essential. (Can you believe my husband, Ethan, thought cooking and cleaning should remain in the essential category?)

Over the next ten years, I memorized the Sermon on the Mount, Ephesians, Philippians, 1 Thessalonians, 2 Timothy, Titus, Hebrews, James, 1 and 2 Peter, 1 John, Revelation, a few Psalms, and other passages.

In order to keep from forgetting these, I set up a schedule to review one book every day, while learning something new. At that time, we didn't have a Christian radio station in Hattiesburg, so instead of what I used to do in Dallas—keep the radio on all day and listen to *someone else teach* what they learned from the Bible—I worked around the house *learning Scripture for myself.* I found it easy to do many activities at the same time, while learning or reviewing Scripture: showering, putting on makeup, vacuuming, folding laundry, cooking, cleaning, washing floors, driving all over town, and many other jobs that don't require thinking.

At the end of each day, physical exhaustion spread over me, but weariness did not. In fact, I felt victorious as I constantly battled the distractions of the day and still squeezed in God's Word. I began connecting the dots between God's requirement of me and the part I'm responsible for. Would God want me to know Him and spend time in His Word, but then make that impossible to achieve? No, but neither does He makes it effortless. He will make a way when I put forth the effort and show my willingness to put Him first.

An aroma of joy permeated my heart and my home. This frazzled mom began to change. An urgency to make up for lost time replaced the guilt caused by spiritual neglect. I had a renewed confidence that God would help me raise my children according to His plan. His presence guided me throughout my day, in every decision, at every turn.

Where did the pursuit of knowledge fit into my understanding? Doesn't the Bible say, "Knowledge makes arrogant, but love edifies" (1 Corinthians 8:1 NASB), and, "If I have . . . all knowledge . . . but do not have love, I am nothing" (1 Corinthians 13:2 NASB)? Knowledge for knowledge's sake couldn't be the answer, but what about 2 Peter 1:3: "everything we need for life and godliness through our knowledge of him"? The answer to this dilemma appears in the same chapter of 2 Peter.

> For this very reason, make every effort to add to your faith goodness; and to goodness, knowledge; and to knowledge, self-control; and to self-control, perseverance; and to perseverance, godliness; and to godliness, brotherly kindness; and to brotherly kindness, love. For if you possess these qualities in increasing measure, they will keep you from being ineffective and unproductive in your knowledge of our Lord Jesus Christ. (2 Peter 1:5–8)

In other words, if you are not growing in your faith—adding to your faith—your knowledge becomes ineffective and unproductive. But if you are continually growing in your faith, your knowledge will have a positive effect. It will keep your knowledge productive and effective. The bottom line: Knowledge is meaningless without application.

People ask me, "What's the most difficult part of memorizing?" The answer? Living it! For example, memorizing book of James put me in a constant state of rebuke because so much in my life needed to be changed. I knew I wasn't living it.

James says, "Do not merely listen to the word, and so deceive yourselves. Do what it says" (James 1:22). That's telling me that if I listen to, or read, or even memorize the Word, but I don't do what it says, then I'm deceived because I think I'm Okay, just fine, doing well, simply because I memorized the Word. James doesn't leave it there. He says that if you listen to the Word but don't do what it says, you're like the person who looks in the mirror, sees his flaws, but goes away forgetting to fix the problem (James 1:23–24). In contrast, the man who looks intently into the Word does not forget what he sees and makes the needed correction. This man will be blessed in whatever he does (see v. 25). The Word of God acts as a mirror, revealing who we are, inside and out.

A friend of mine, Beverly, worked with me years ago, volunteering at our children's school. One day Beverly came to school to help out. She'd been there for several hours and then went to the ladies' room. As she leaned over to wash her hands, she noticed in the mirror that she still had a curler on top of her head. She'd been walking around school with that curler on her head, and no one told her about it. But the mirror told her. Now, what do you suppose was the likelihood that after seeing the curler she left it there and walked away? None. She yanked it out immediately.

Two important factors emerge from this story: knowledge and application. Beverly worked at the school for several hours with no knowledge of the problem, so how could she take action? As soon as the mirror showed her the truth, she made the needed correction. So it is with God's Word. Application is vital, but we cannot apply what we do not know.

The connection between knowledge and application became clearer in my own life. Knowledge is meaningless without application, but you won't have application if you don't have knowledge.

God provided many opportunities in my own home to apply the knowledge I gained. But it wasn't as smooth sailing as it may have appeared from the outside. The more I got into God's Word, the more knowledge I acquired, and the more I felt compelled to apply it. But this became a heavy burden to me because I exposed myself to so much. For example, memorizing the Sermon on the Mount (Matthew 5–7) nailed me with humanly impossible teachings. Jesus said:

> But I tell you: Love your enemies and pray for those who persecute you, that you may be sons of your Father in heaven. He causes his sun to rise on the evil and the good, and sends rain on the righteous and the unrighteous. If you love those who love you, what reward will you get? Are not even the tax collectors doing that? And if you greet only your brothers, what are you doing more than others? Do not even pagans do that? (Matthew 5:44–47)

Such powerful words and a call to a lifestyle so far from my own! I struggled to love everyday people, and now I was supposed to love my enemies?

Why did God give me His Word if it only pointed out my inadequacies and failure to live up to its principles? My own knowledge overwhelmed me! My constant prayer was, "Lord, I want to go beyond knowledge. I don't want to be one of those people who can quote the Bible but whose life disgraces the cause of Christ. O God, I'd rather die than be that person."

The Lord knew my quandary, but He had already shown me the answer in the book of Ephesians. How quickly I'd forgotten! Notice the word *power* throughout Paul's prayer for the Ephesians.

> For this reason I kneel before the Father, from whom his whole family in heaven and on earth derives its name. I pray that out of his glorious riches he may strengthen you with *power* through his Spirit in your inner being, so that Christ may dwell in your hearts through faith. And I pray that you, being rooted and established in love, may have *power*, together with all the saints, to grasp how wide and long and high and deep is the love of Christ, and to know this love that surpasses knowledge—that you may be filled to the measure of all the fullness of God. Now to him who is able to do immeasurably more than all we ask or imagine, according to his *power* that is at work within us, to him be glory in the church and in Christ Jesus throughout all generations, for ever and ever! Amen. (Ephesians 3:14–21, emphasis added)

God alone gives the power to know the depth and breadth of His love, and only experientially knowing the love of Christ will surpass knowledge. On my own I am incapable of living up to His Word. God's power, working in me and through me, will enable me to go beyond knowledge.

Step by step, God was leading me in my understanding, teaching me what it meant to really know Him and walk with Him. I had tasted knowledge and found it delightfully satisfying. I'd also become aware of the need to make knowledge more than word intake. I see now that God had me right where He wanted me. He was beginning to write His Word in my heart.

2» MY GOALS: THEN & NOW

DURING MY TEENAGE YEARS, my family lived on a lake in Winter Park, Florida. In the backyard, we had a cypress tree that lived right at the water's edge. It became a favorite place to sit and talk, or just rest, watching the waves splash up against the tree. Even in the scorching Florida sun, that tree was never parched; the water was its life source. In contrast, we had a huge oak tree in the front yard covered with thick Spanish moss. This grand, stately tree lost branches every year because the moss began to take over. This picture of two contrasting trees presents a parallel for us: One tree thrives while the other withers. And what will be the deciding factor as to which tree my life resembles? It will depend on what I allow as the dominant influence in my life.

Psalm 1 compares a certain man to a flourishing tree.

Blessed is the man
    who does not walk in the counsel of the wicked
or stand in the way of sinners
    or sit in the seat of mockers.
But his delight is in the law of the Lord,
    and on his law he meditates day and night.
He is like a tree planted by streams of water,
    which yields its fruit in season

and whose leaf does not wither.

Whatever he does prospers. (Psalm 1:1–3)

What kind of person does *God* call blessed? One not swayed by ungodly men but whose influence comes from meditating on God's Word day and night. How does God describe that person? "Like a tree planted by streams of water," continually nourished, never thirsty. This person yields fruit in season, according to God's timing. Because his mind and heart delight in God's Word, his actions are God-centered and divinely prosperous.

In the previous chapter, I told you how the apostle Peter challenged my thinking by asserting that God had given me everything I needed for life and godliness through my knowledge of Him. Grace and peace would be mine in abundance *through* my knowledge of Him. God gave me His Word so that I might *know* Him. Could this be why the psalmist decreed a blessing on the man who would meditate on God's law day and night? I see the connection as both obvious and profound. The one who meditates on God's Word day and night will have an increasing knowledge of God, and in knowing Him, he will have everything he needs for life and godliness. He will prosper in all that he does. Why? He prospers because, as he is watered and nourished by the Word, he begins to live out what he takes in and a fruitful life emerges. No wonder he is called "blessed."

The first few years that I memorized passages, my enthusiasm caused me to wonder why every Christian didn't memorize books and passages. Maybe God left it optional. I began to investigate. I went to the Bible first. Was there a command to memorize Scripture? I couldn't locate one. I couldn't even find the word *memorize*. I searched even the Greek and the Hebrew and couldn't find a word that meant to *memorize*. Do I hear a sigh of relief out there? The Bible does *not* command us to memorize Scripture. Having said that, these commands and exhortations do apply to each of us.

- Know God's Word.
- Remember God's Word.
- Do not forget His commandments.
- Have His Word ready on your lips.
- Meditate on His law day and night.
- Dwell on Christ's words.
- Store up His words.
- Keep God's Word within your heart.

For me, memorizing passages provides a way to accomplish those objectives. God desires for us to know Him intimately and to follow Him correctly—that's why He gave us His written Word. The Bible, God's revelation of Himself, leaves nothing out that He wants us to know. Spending quality time in God's Word leads us to a greater knowledge of God, and memorizing is one productive way to achieve that. The goal of memorizing should not be confused with the ultimate goal of knowing God and loving Him.

Consider these words of Moses: "Fix these words of mine in your hearts and minds; tie them as symbols on your hands and bind them on your foreheads" (Deuteronomy 11:18). Moses exhorts us to make sure God's words are written on our hearts and minds. We must impress them into the very core of our lives and make them as permanent as possible.

The reference to binding words to the hands and forehead

can be interpreted symbolically as all of your actions (your hands) and all of your thoughts (your forehead). God's Word must be central in all that we are, all that we do, and all that we think about. *We must do whatever it takes* to keep God foremost in our lives. A healthy combination includes reading God's Word, listening to it, studying, teaching, meditating and thinking about it, and memorizing God's Word.

I know many godly men and women who do not memorize God's Word. Through study and meditation they keep the Bible at the center of their lives. In my own life, however, profound changes occurred when I began to memorize passages of Scripture, and I can't keep silent about the impact.

Since God directs us to meditate on His Word day and night, what exactly does that look like? Our common understanding of meditation is to think deeply about something, to ponder, to contemplate. An accurate understanding of the biblical term requires digging into the Old Testament. The Hebrew transliteration of the term is *haghah*. Literally it means "to murmur; to mutter; to sigh; to moan; to muse; to speak; to whisper."[1] Did you notice that these terms involve making sounds with your mouth, speaking words quietly to yourself? This new insight reveals to us that our biblical instruction goes beyond just *thinking* about God's Word and extends to actually *saying the words out loud*.

A conventional teaching technique employed universally combines seeing, hearing, and speaking to augment the learning process. Meditation involves all three. As we see and say and hear the words over and over, we allow the transforming power of God's Word to alter our thinking, our behavior, and our very lives.

In the twenty references on meditation given in the

Psalms, what was the psalmist meditating on? God's Word, God's work, God's ways, God's wonders. Those things the Israelites rehearsed with their minds and their lips. For me, memorizing Scripture has become an act of worship. It ushers me into God's presence and keeps me spiritually renewed each day. As a busy wife and mother, with an entire household affected by my demeanor, I cannot afford to miss a single day of fellowship with God; the consequences are too far-reaching.

In many of the religions that have permeated our society, meditation involves emptying your mind for the purpose of relaxation, detoxifying your body and soul, and relieving stress. In contrast, the biblical concept of meditation is to fill your mind with God's thoughts and character and purposes. I can't think of any greater stress relief than to commune with God, free from bondage to myself and to the world's philosophies.

If you've had good results from meditating on Scripture *without* memorizing it, you are a rare breed, an exception to the norm. For most of us, the problem with meditating begins when a great thought gets morphed into our list of things to do, phone calls we need to make, etc. Distraction comes easily without something specific to focus on.

For example, you might choose to meditate on the love of God—a broad and general topic. Where do your thoughts begin, and then where do they go? Recalling a Scripture helps you zoom in on specifics: "How great is the love the Father has lavished on us, that we should be called children of God! And that is what we are!" (1 John 3:1). Now you have substance rather than a generic thought, and much to consider concerning the love of God.

Memorizing passages gives meditation a specific target, specific thoughts, specific words.

I advocate memorizing passages and books instead of scattered, disconnected verses. Memorizing passages, chapters, or entire books far exceeds the benefit of memorizing seventy-five independent verses. If one of your goals is to grow in your understanding of God, then you will get a more complete picture if you memorize verses that go together. For example, the book of Philippians contains God's unified message to the church at Philippi. The book of Galatians contains God's unified message to the churches in the region of Galatia. God's ideas for each remain intact without interruption.

Many individual verses, when memorized out of context, can give a false meaning. Would you be surprised to know that one verse, John 3:16, has given many people a false assurance of their salvation? How could this be? Because they don't understand the word *believe*. If they knew John chapter 3 in its entirety, they would know that

- you must be born again (verses 3–7);
- those who know and believe the truth will have deeds that prove their belief (verses 19–21);
- those who believe have eternal life; but those who do not obey the Son of God shall not see life but God's wrath abides on them (verse 36).

Memorizing verses 1–21 gives the entire conversation between Jesus and Nicodemus, and the chapter helps avoid a misinterpretation of John 3:16. Most verses depend on supporting verses in order to get an accurate interpretation. By memorizing sequential verses you avoid wrong thinking, which leads to wrong application.

Have you ever noticed that individual verses we choose to

memorize are often self-focused? We're looking for what we can get from God. For example,

> Delight yourself in the Lord, and He will give you the desires of your heart. (Psalm 37:4 NASB)
> And my God will supply all your needs according to His riches in glory in Christ Jesus. (Philippians 4:19 NASB)
> No good thing does He withhold from those who walk uprightly. (Psalm 84:11 NASB)
> He who did not spare His own Son, but delivered Him over for us all, how will He not also with Him freely give us all things? (Romans 8:32 NASB)

I memorized each of these verses years ago as a new Christian, so that I could be sure God would give me everything I needed and wanted. The verses focused on *me*. A better approach involves memorizing them in their context, which keeps the focus on God and greatly enhances our learning in the process. God put His thoughts and His words in a particular order within each book and never intended for us to cut-and-paste the sections we like.

The challenge of memorizing large portions—whole chapters or entire books—seems to intimidate people. They think it will be more difficult or time-consuming than memorizing independent verses. Let me tell you about a man in my church in Mississippi. He told me that his goal for the year was to memorize Philippians. He counted the 104 verses and divided them into 52 weeks, coming up with his plan of two verses a week. Now does that sound overwhelmingly difficult or time-consuming? Two verses a week was a manageable goal for him.

If he accomplished his goal—and I hope he did—then he would be motivated the next year to take on another book. Many books in the New Testament contain approximately the same number of verses, so at the same pace of two verses a week, he could have five books memorized in five years, and ten books memorized in ten years—at two verses a week. That doesn't seem possible, but you can do the math. Just a few verses a week adds up to a lot of Scripture. In the next chapter, I will teach you my method, and then you can adapt it to suit you, as this man did.

By far, the keystone in memorizing is reviewing. Without review you lose everything you memorize. For this reason, passages are much simpler because you can review an entire chapter, about twenty-one verses, in less than three minutes, without stopping to name the references. When you memorize a passage or a book, you don't need to memorize the references. (The number-one reason people don't enjoy memorizing Scripture is because they have trouble with the references.) You also gain God's unified flow of thought as His Word unfolds.

The time factor usually surprises people who hear about my Scripture memory accomplishments. Contrary to what most people think, it takes very little time to memorize Scripture because you can do it while you do other things. Because of the value of God's Word in my life, I don't want to go a single day without spending time in the Word. But a goal of studying the Bible every day has never worked realistically for me. I suppose if I had no husband and no job and lived in a full-service hotel, I could manage to study the Bible every day. My jam-packed life probably resembles yours—with never-ending activity from dawn to dusk. On many days, life's demands keep me so consumed that I fall into bed exhausted and have not opened my Bible all day. But, thanks to memorizing Scripture, it's a very rare day when I've not spent time in God's Word. The habit of memorizing and reviewing throughout my day keeps me in God's Word.

People ask if it's my goal to memorize the whole Bible. I tell them no. That's not what they're expecting. Honestly, I have no aspirations of becoming the Bible trivia queen or even the Bible answer woman. I want God's Word written on my heart so that my life reflects a close walk with God.

For more than ten years an uncomplicated goal motivated my daily Scripture intake: to know God and walk closely with Him. Simple, uncluttered, focused. In the midst of the daily grind, I aimed for joy—and found it in God-breathed words.

Memorizing Scripture was not a search for answers to all the tough questions, not for intellectual enhancement, nor to impress anyone beyond the confines of my own dwelling. I had no visions of influence outside my little nest, aspiring only to be a mother who communes with God. I knew my children would benefit from that foundation. As God's Word permeated my mind and heart I weathered the storms of each day—the disappointments, the setbacks, the aggravations. My anxious heart settled down and embraced this child-raising interval.

Though I pursued avenues to serve God and help others, those were not reasons why I memorized Scripture. I knew the verse that instructs, "Always be ready to give an answer" (1 Peter 3:15), but I was not driven by it.

At that season of my life, I concentrated first on *me*, never mind trying to change the world or even make a dent. I knew that if my soul thrived everything else would fall into place. I had to begin there. Above everything else, I wanted to know God and walk closely with Him. This simple goal dominated my thinking.

As the years progressed, the Lord broadened my perspective and widened my sphere. His Word in my heart had given me a vantage point from which to view the world. There were so many hurting, joyless people, and I held a prescription for weariness in my own hands.

As I beat the drum to my favorite mantra, *everything for life and godliness*, I realized more and more that godliness—that is, being like God—means, in part, doing what God does. And what does God do? He spreads His name and His kingdom throughout the earth. He uses people and situations to reveal Himself and His redemptive purpose in the world.

Before I had children, I had served in ministry full-time; there was a six-year gap between graduating from college and having children. A lot of my satisfaction in life was wrapped up in being usable by God. When my children arrived, somehow motherhood made me feel like I was on hold in God's service and would be reconnected later, after my children went off to school.

As I see it now looking back, I realize that God wanted me to be a teacher of His Word. But I didn't know the Word, so what was He going to do, send me out to teach heresy? The sobering truth was that I had already been teaching Bible studies for years. Yikes!

Somewhere in God's grand scheme He prepared me as His workmanship and created me to do good works. An increasing desire to participate more fully in God's agenda stretched my focal point. I wanted my life centered on His kingdom, not mine. My goal in memorizing expanded.

I had a continuing hunger to know more and a drive to pass on what I learned, both from the text and from daily life. I wanted to be that "instrument for noble purposes, made holy, useful to the Master and prepared to do any good work" (2 Timothy 2:21).

For fourteen years I taught God's Word at a weekly Precept Bible study, and an increasing number of invitations came to speak at women's events—huge responsibilities for which I desired to be better equipped.

My daughter, finally grown, headed east to college, and three years later my son headed south—an empty nest so soon. Tears and joy juxtaposed, sadness and delight in the same sandwich.

Ten days after my son left, Hurricane Katrina arrived in south Mississippi. No electricity for fourteen days, hot nights with no fans, sweating through every pore. Days were spent in manual cleanup, waiting in the Red Cross line, and bidding for laborers. Evenings had few options, so Ethan and I dreamed out loud, just the two of us.

Where would life take us in this new phase? Ethan asked, "What do you want to do with your life now that the kids are gone?" At fifty years old, I anticipated the new adventures that waited for me. I vocalized my growing fantasy: "I really want to go to seminary." I'd expressed these thoughts before, but now it seemed like possibilities could come true.

God's Word had awakened within me a love of learning and an excitement about maximizing whatever years I had left. We explored various options and settled on Dallas Theological Seminary. Once more, moving trucks stuffed, a memory-filled house emptied, and the second half of a round-trip taken. My journey came full circle. Sixteen years in Mississippi, then back to Dallas. Strange, but God had fulfilled the purpose He had for me in Mississippi. I didn't view it as a sixteen-year detour, but rather another fork in the road designed by God.

A four-year masters of theology turned into five and a half years—I had to squeeze in a Mississippi wedding for my daughter. More years down the road, I now have two granddaughters, and the life cycle begins anew.

My goal in memorizing Scripture evolved beyond myself. The next generation is counting on Gran Jan.

My advice to you, however, has not changed. Don't memorize Scripture for someone else; do it for you. Don't change the waking minutes of your day just so that you have an answer for someone else. Change the way you spend your time so that you will know God and walk closely with Him. An empty vessel has nothing to give. A bubbling fountain splashes everyone close to it.

Blessed is the man who meditates on God's Word day and night. He chooses to make God the major influence in his life, and this counteracts the pull of the world. Like a tree near the water, his thirsty soul drinks freely and branches out with luscious fruit.

3»
YOUR TURN: TAKE THE PLUNGE

TODAY AN EXPERIMENT awaits you. It's your turn to see what memorizing God's Word can do for you. I always recommend that you start out with something very small, so that you will get a taste without a huge commitment. I started with Ephesians, but I don't recommend it. Psalm 1 is a perfect place to start. It's concise, only six verses, and most important, it paints a portrait of a blessed man who meditates on God's Word day and night.

If you already know Psalm 1 by heart, let me suggest Psalm 121. It is eight verses long, and its theme is God watching over us. Other options might be Psalm 4, Psalm 8, Psalm 23, or Psalm 100.

People often ask me if I have a great method for memorizing Scripture. I tell them, "You don't need a great method as much as you need great motivation. If you're highly motivated, any method will do." My simple approach will get you started.

Two things before we begin: Choose a version of the Bible that you like best. It will be easier if you choose the one you're most familiar with. I always memorize in the New International Version-1984, but I study and teach from the New American Standard Bible. This gets confusing sometimes, so I don't recommend it. It will be less complicated if you stick with the Scripture version you know best. Avoid paraphrases because they are not accurate translations but influenced by someone's opinions. If you're going to put some effort into this, you may as well get the genuine article. Don't forget that inherent in God's Word is the power to transform your life. That's why we're doing this.

Second, choose how you will access the Bible verses you want to memorize. There are many options. When I began memorizing more than twenty years ago, I used to write out my verses on 3 x 5 index cards, held together on a spiral, which kept them organized and not scattered all over my house. I bought these spirals, containing fifty index cards, at the grocery or office supply store. The spiral sits easily on any counter in my house, and I can take it with me anywhere.

The twenty-first century gives us many more options. A Bible app on your phone works well because you can take it with you easily. The Bible is also available on all notebooks and tablets. For easy access, you can bookmark the passage you're working on.

What you want is something you can take with you easily. Carrying your Bible everywhere isn't practical. Another easy option is to go to a Bible website, like Biblegateway.com and print out the passage in the version you like. You can choose font size, which helps me as I get older. After a few months when the pages get worn out, just go back and reprint.

A creature of habit, I still write out my verses on an index-card spiral. I can usually fit up to ten chapters on one spiral. No battery to recharge and no excuses. I also print the passage from my computer. My iPad usually sits in my office and can be accessed instantly. I have my Bible app set on 2 Thessalonians, which is my most recent passage.

If you choose to write out your verses, copy them one

phrase per line (if it fits) because we will learn it this way. When I write out my verses I put the reference number on the left of each new verse, but I never memorize the numbers, nor do I recommend it.

Do not lose sight of your goal. It's not the memorization itself that is important but the constant reflection on God, His character and His ways. The psalmist writes, "Seven times a day I praise you for your righteous laws" (Psalm 119:164). The number seven is not suggesting an exact number but rather a continual turning to God's Word throughout the day. With this in mind, you're ready to begin.

Day 1

— ◆ —

PSALM 1:1

Blessed is the man who does not walk
in the counsel of the wicked or stand in the way
of sinners or sit in the seat of mockers.

- ◆ I like to begin first thing in the morning, but let's not wait.
- ◆ Go ahead and try this one verse. Take it phrase by phrase, line by line. See how far you can get.
- ◆ Concentrate on the verse. Say it out loud, over and over.
- ◆ It takes less than ten seconds to say this one verse. You can fit that in just about anywhere.
- ◆ How many times today can you review this verse? At least a dozen times.
- ◆ Have your verses within reach wherever you go: into the kitchen, driving in your car.
- ◆ Say your verses while doing other things: chores, errands, waiting, exercising.

◆ Ask, "Who is God calling blessed?" This psalm begins by saying what the blessed man does not do.

◆ Come back to this verse throughout your day: mid-morning, afternoon stretch, evening.

◆ Focus on what is being said. Evaluate your own life. Does this describe you?

◆ Take the last few minutes of your day to review and reflect.

◆ Ask God to give you an expectant heart as you learn these verses.

Day 2
— ◆ —

PSALM 1:2

But his delight is in the law of the Lord,
and on his law he meditates day and night.

◆ Begin reviewing verse 1 first thing in the morning. Say it in the shower.

◆ See if you can remember the verse without looking.

◆ Move on to verse 2. Say them both together. Repeat the two verses out loud.

◆ Now you're up to about fifteen seconds. I told you it doesn't take a lot of time.

◆ The psalm now tells us what the blessed man does.

◆ Think about the verse and the man. Notice the contrast between verses 1 and 2.

◆ What does it mean to delight in God's law? Does this verse describe you? Do you want it to?

◆ Take your verses with you everywhere. Have them only a click away on your phone.

◆ Put the verses on the counter when you're making breakfast, coffee, and school lunches.

◆ Review while you drive in your car or ride public transportation.

◆ Turn the radio off and let your mind dwell on these truths.

◆ Before you go to bed, sit still, review your verses, and make them a prayer to God.

Day 3

◆

PSALM 1:3

He is like a tree planted by streams of water,
which yields its fruit in season
and whose leaf does not wither.
Whatever he does prospers.

◆ Start your day by reviewing your first two verses.

◆ If you reviewed the verses fifteen or twenty times yesterday, they should come right back to you.

◆ Your biggest block of time is probably while getting ready for the day.

◆ Share the verse with a friend, your spouse, your kids, or with the mirror. It all works.

◆ Think about today's verse. How is the man described? What characterizes his life?

◆ How is it possible that whatever he does prospers? Does this happen overnight or does it take time? Meditate on the connection.

◆ You are now up to about twenty-five seconds of review time. What a great way to spend twenty-five seconds!

◆ Say the three verses throughout your day. Fit in review whenever you can.

- Household chores are not so laborious when you add Scripture: vacuuming, unloading the dishwasher, folding laundry, sweeping the front porch, even taking out the garbage.

- Before you go to bed, fill your mind with God's words.

- Surrender your heart and life afresh to God. Ask Him to write these words on your heart.

Day 4

— ◆ —

PSALM 1:4

Not so the wicked!
They are like chaff that the wind blows away.

- As soon as you wake up, begin reviewing your first three verses out loud.

- Add today's verse. Review all four together. You'll be up to thirty seconds review time.

- Say these four verses ten or more times while getting ready for your day.

- Think about the new verse. Say it out loud, over and over.

- What is "not so" about the wicked? They do not prosper.

- Why not? Because they are like chaff that the wind blows away.

- What is chaff? It's the useless part of the grain that comes off during threshing.

- Take your verses with you and practice them while you run errands.

- Look over the verses while you're waiting at the bank drive-thru, piano lessons, soccer practice.

- You have a few seconds while waiting for the elevator and the copy machine. A lot of precious time can be redeemed while waiting.

◆ Before going to bed, review a few times. Trust God to make these words a reality in your life.

Day 5

—— ◆ ——

PSALM 1:5

Therefore the wicked will not stand in the judgment,
nor sinners in the assembly of the righteous.

◆ When the alarm clock sounds, begin reviewing your four verses. You've got the hang of it now.

◆ Add verse 5 and review them all together. You're up to thirty-five seconds now.

◆ Repeat your verses while making breakfast and throwing clothes in the laundry.

◆ Share your verses with your spouse and kids, even the cat.

◆ Review while you drive to work or school.

◆ Meditate on what today's verse means. It's a conclusion, a summary statement.

◆ There is a day of reckoning coming. You want to be one who is standing.

◆ Come back to your verses at lunch or during a work break.

◆ Review while cooking dinner and doing the dishes.

◆ Take a reflective moment before bedtime, and think of the joy you've experienced today.

Day 6

PSALM 1:6

For the Lord watches over the way of the righteous,
but the way of the wicked will perish.

◆ Give your first thoughts of the day to reviewing your five verses. Can you do it without looking?

◆ Add today's verse. Say it out loud, over and over and over. Concentrate.

◆ Keep reviewing throughout the day.

◆ The forty seconds for this psalm are time well spent.

◆ Think about this final verse. The Lord watches over you. What a comforting thought.

◆ Ask yourself the hard questions: *Does this psalm call for a change in my life?*

◆ Do you want to be the one who God calls "blessed"? Now you know how. Go after it.

◆ You're already on your way. Ask God to help you develop good habits.

◆ Train your mind to run to God's Word throughout the day.

◆ Practice these verses whenever you can squeeze in forty seconds.

◆ Rehearse the words while walking the dog, picking up around the house or yard.

◆ Save the last few minutes of your day to thank God for His words of life.

Day 7

PSALM I

- ◆ Start the day by reviewing all of Psalm I. Go over it several times out loud.
- ◆ Thank God for His faithfulness in helping you absorb His Word.
- ◆ Say your verses throughout the house, in your car, and everywhere you go.
- ◆ Call a friend and bless his or her day with these verses.
- ◆ You have been meditating on God's Word day and night for seven days. How does it feel?
- ◆ Relish the joy of a goal accomplished. Congratulate yourself. Your Father is well pleased.
- ◆ Ask God to stir your heart with a longing for more truth.
- ◆ Make your final review before bed, taking time to reflect on your journey this week.
- ◆ Determine within you to stay in God's Word and truly make His Word your delight.

Look back over the seven days and evaluate. What encourages you? How is your outlook on life? Have you found more free moments than you thought you had? Are there more to be captured? Do you feel nourished and sustained? Strengthened and fortified? Is God true to His Word? Yes, always. You've tasted the sweetness. You've taken the plunge. Now keep going!

Now that you have Psalm 1 in your mind, how will you make sure you will not forget what you have worked so diligently to remember? In chapter 9, I will cover review strategies, but let me get you started now. Pick a certain day of the week, let's say Friday, on which you will always review Psalm 1. No matter what else you go on to memorize, every Friday you will review Psalm 1. Remember, it only takes forty seconds to review, so this is doable. If it doesn't come back smoothly, spend some more time working on it before you move on to your next project. At the end of a year, you will have reviewed the psalm at least fifty-two times. This process will move it from short-term memory to long-term memory, so that you will never, ever forget it.

For some of you, the pace of one verse a day has been too slow. You're hungry and eager to tackle more verses in a shorter period of time. Don't let me hold you back. Do as much as you are comfortable with. Your goal should be to find the pace that keeps you meditating on God's Word all day long. I recommend at least a verse a day in order to discipline your mind. For example, if you only attempt one verse per week, that does not force you to keep bringing your thoughts back to God throughout the day. When I first began memorizing, I took on more verses in a week's time than I do presently. And yet the total time spent meditating is probably about the same. It's just that now I'm devoting a part of each day to reviewing my other passages.

For some of you, a verse a day overwhelms you and you need a slower pace. Adapt my method to what works for you.

In chapter 5, we will tackle a new passage, now that you have conquered Psalm 1. Don't be intimidated. Longer passages are not more difficult; they just take longer. You learn every passage the exact same way.

Some people think I must have a photographic memory. Unfortunately for me, I don't. My two children, now grown, would love to tell you their mother is not the sharpest pencil in the drawer. When it came to helping with homework, I could never remember any history, any geometry, any science, or any other subject—no Jeopardy champion here! So why have I been so successful at memorizing Scripture? It's because I have a higher goal than just memorizing the Bible. My primary goal is to know God and walk closely with Him. I've chosen to make this discipline one of the joyful habits in my life.

To ensure that you will keep meditating on God's Word day and night, train yourself to recognize any pockets of time in your day that you can fill with God's Word. You may be waiting at the haircutters and they are backed up. Learn to grab those moments. You take your car for an oil change or a car wash, and those valuable moments turn into extra moments for God's Word.

Identify activities that already take up dead time. Do you play games on your phone while waiting? Are you an Angry Birds addict? Do Sudoku puzzles keep you busy in airports or train stations? Do you read magazines in the carpool line? Oh, and how about Pinterest? Many an idle evening gets swallowed up there. I haven't even hinted at (until now) the wasted hours on Facebook and Twitter. Most people have routines, even for dead time. Ask God to help you change your routines, allowing more time for Him.

Here's another suggestion: Set up signals for yourself as reminders to go over your verse for the day:

- If you have a smartphone, you can program an alarm one time and it will go off every day at the designated times, such as 10 a.m., 12 p.m., 2 p.m., and 4 p.m. This will remind you every two hours to go over your verse for the day, setting up a habit that you will do automatically, without prompting, later.

- If you are a morning and afternoon coffee drinker, go over the day's verse while your coffee is brewing.
- Pick parts of your daily routine and incorporate Scripture memory into those things.

About ten years ago, I met Kent Shaw while speaking at a women's conference at Harvest Bible Chapel, where he is on staff. He was memorizing the Sermon on the Mount at the time. I emailed him a few weeks ago and asked if he was still memorizing, and if he would share with my readers the benefit he receives and some of his method. His response follows.

Janet,

Yes, I am still actively memorizing the Word of God. I couldn't live without it! Memorizing the Word is one of the best of all spiritual disciplines because it combines meditation, prayer, and the study of God's Word. I earnestly desire to be a Psalm 1 man, and there is no better way than memorizing the Word. I believe actively and aggressively meditating on the Word will radically change your life. It will fill your heart with faith, hope, and love. It will bring enormous joy and peace into your life because God's Word is alive, active, and powerful!

I memorize one verse a day, and after I finish a chapter I spend a few days reviewing the previous chapters. I memorize with my twenty-six-year-old daughter, and we occasionally quiz each other. So far, after ten years, I have memorized the Sermon on the Mount, the Gospel of John, Romans, 2 Corinthians,

Galatians, Hebrews, James, and several chapters in Psalms and Proverbs.

I try to give myself two hours in the morning to spend in the Word. As I am memorizing the verse of the day, I have a study Bible and commentary so I can study the passage in more detail as I memorize it. I then pray the passage back to the Lord and try to meditate on the Word throughout the day. Some days are better than others. I try to make my last thoughts of the day before I go to sleep meditating on the Word.

I don't have a sophisticated system of memorizing the Word. I have found that if you are sold on the value and see the importance of something, you will put in the work to gain the benefit.

Kent C. Shaw

Executive Director, Harvest Bible Fellowship

Well, blow me away! I think we've found a Psalm-1 man in the twenty-first century.

4》 THE BENEFITS OF KNOWLEDGE

MARTIN LUTHER, A PRIEST in the sixteenth century, altered his theology and mission when he fully grasped the meaning of Romans 1:17, "The just shall live by faith" (KJV). On the basis of that single verse, he led the Protestant Reformation and pointed the world to salvation by grace, through faith and not by works. Can one verse of Scripture change the course of a person's life? Yes, it can, and such was the case for me with this verse: "His divine power has given us everything we need for life and godliness through our knowledge of him" (2 Peter 1:3).

I have only begun to tell you the profound impression this one verse has made on my approach to life and the direction I have taken. I made a conscious decision: I chose to take God at His Word, and it compelled me to travel on a different route. I changed my focus and deliberately pursued the knowledge of God, with no reserve and no Plan B. If this declaration from God, "Everything we need for life and godliness," was true, then it was surely the most fantastic promise in the Bible, and I wasn't going to miss out on it. Though I have no plans of starting any Reformation, I am nonetheless burdened to convince the Christian world of the implications of this one verse.

As I gave careful attention to the Word, my knowledge of God compounded daily. But did I get everything I needed for life and godliness? Strangely enough, as the months and years went by, I never stopped to wonder what those things were. I just knew that He would provide them. Looking back, I see that God began with my greatest need.

A meaningful, adoring relationship with the One I call Lord and Father will always be my most indispensable need. The opportunity to commune with God, relating to Him as a child with her daddy or as a devoted servant with a loving master, enriches my existence. Through His Word I've found increasing joy in His companionship and a gratified heart that seeks no other source. His Word ushers me into His presence and feeds me at His table. This has been, by far, the greatest benefit of knowing God's Word. If to know Him is to love Him, then to know Him greatly is to love Him greatly.

Why should I find it so astounding that my greatest need came from His greatest command? His preeminent requirement of me was the thing I needed most. When Jesus was asked, "Which is the quintessential commandment?" He answered, "Love the Lord your God with all your heart and with all your soul and with all your mind and with all your strength" (Mark 12:28–30). God's utmost desire for you and me is that we love Him. And what we need most for life and godliness is an abiding love relationship with God.

The very inclusion of the word *all*—all your heart, all your soul, all your mind, and all your strength—makes clear that Jesus specifies a progressive love, one that involves more and more, not less and less, until every aspect of our being belongs to Him. God asks a lot of us. Why? Because the totality of our life flows from that relationship. Everything we attempt to do in serving God and serving others springs from God's preeminence in our lives.

But how can we fulfill this supreme command to love God if we don't know the Object of our affection? How can we love God if we don't know Him? And what about the intensity of love demanded? If our knowledge of God is shallow, can our love be deep?

For years I short-circuited my relationship with God without realizing it. By not going deeper into His Word, I was not accelerating my knowledge of God, and consequently my love for God was less than it could be. I didn't love God more because I wasn't getting to know Him more.

As I devoted myself to pursuing the knowledge of God, my heart drew closer to His. The apostle John tells us, "We love [God] because he first loved us" (1 John 4:19). This is true. Our love for God is in response to His abundant love for us. He was and is the initiator of our relationship. Now I can see why Paul prayed that we would know the depth and breadth of the love of God, for only then can we love Him in return. I don't think it ever registered in my brain that my love for God would depend on my knowledge of His love for me. But sure enough, the more I knew Him, the more I loved Him. How simple it all seems now, so elementary, to say that my greatest need for life and godliness was to love God more.

In terms of human relationships, one might easily conclude that if you want to love someone more you must get to know that person more. That doesn't sound complicated, but we often overlook this in our relationship with God. And how did God devise for us to know Him? He gave us His written Word. That was His plan. The Scriptures contain everything God wants us to know about Him. The Bible is God's complete message to His beloved children. He gave us His Word so that we can know Him.

Then why are we looking in so many other places? On occasion, I've heard Christians say, "I get to know God best in nature." The problem with that statement is that if nature is all you have, then you are missing out on the depth of understanding He intends for you to have toward Him. God gave even unbelievers revelation in nature. If you only pursue God in nature, you'll end up settling for the unbelievers' portion.

We'll never be satisfied with a universal knowledge of God. We want a personal knowledge, a relational knowledge, because God is a relational being, not just an energy force in the cosmos. God desires a personal relationship, and that's why He gave His Book to His children.

After telling a parable to the multitudes, the disciples asked Jesus, "Why do you speak to the people in parables?" Jesus replied, "The knowledge of the secrets of the kingdom of heaven has been given to you, but not to them" (Matthew 13:10–11). Do you hear what Jesus is saying? The knowledge of the secrets of the kingdom of heaven has been given to us. These secrets are ours. They belong to us. What are we doing with them? Do we even know what they are? Do we want to know the secrets of the kingdom of heaven? They're found in God's Word.

There is one more verse I must include: "He who forms the mountains, creates the wind, and *reveals his thoughts to man*, he who turns dawn to darkness, and treads the high places of the earth—the Lord Almighty is his name" (Amos 4:13, emphasis added).

The same God who created the mountains and the wind has chosen to reveal His thoughts to humankind. Why? Because He wants us to know Him! Where has God revealed these thoughts? In the pages of the Bible. So why do we want to find God our own way instead of the way He has chosen to reveal Himself? Our depraved nature, I suppose.

Some even make the Bible their last resort. They'd rather learn about God from their pastor, a radio preacher, worship songs, or a suspenseful Christian novel. I know—been there, done that. Many rob themselves of intimacy with God because they choose to learn vicariously through someone else's study.

As we get to know God one-on-one, we have an inside track on becoming His friend. On the night Jesus was betrayed, He gathered with His disciples, and told them, "I no longer call you servants, because a servant does not know his master's business. Instead, I have called you friends, for everything that I learned from my Father I have made known to you" (John 15:15). What reason did Jesus give for now calling His disciples friends? Because He had told them everything about the family business. He had shared with them His background and His future. He'd revealed His mission and the calling on His life. He had given them knowledge. That was the difference.

My closest friends have the inside scoop on me. They know what makes me tick and what rattles my cage. They know I love watching football games and have no interest in gardening. They know that I could live on coffee and dessert. They know my thoughts and secrets. The closer the friend, the more she knows. My friends know me because I have let them in. I have chosen to reveal myself to them. No one can be my friend unless I give that person access.

We know from the Bible that God chose to reveal Himself to certain people, such as Abraham, Moses, and David. Not only did they know about God, they experienced companionship with God. They walked with God, and His presence was manifested to them. This was God's doing. He chose to let them know Him, to let them be acquainted with Him. And their lives were unique because they knew God as one knows a friend.

Jesus said, "You are my friends if you do what I command" (John 15:14). Years ago, I would have been reluctant to call myself God's friend. It seems so presumptuous, so bold. But now I wouldn't hesitate because I know Him and I am obeying Him. Rather than being arrogant or audacious, I take Him at His Word. He calls me friend, and so I am.

Jesus invites me into a tight relationship with Him. As my closest confidant, He lets me pour out my heart to Him and He discloses His heart to me. He reveals His thoughts page after page. He wrote down His expressions of love for me, His intentions for my highest good, and His unwavering commitment to my future. Secure in His love and provision, I'm free to make my life about Him and not about myself. I don't have to zero in on my needs and pursue my own happiness. I've found more than I bargained for, and I'm not looking elsewhere.

Memorizing Scripture points me to God's character, my need, and the safety of being with Him. Each year brings new challenges, both sorrow and sadness, and inexplicable circumstances. In the midst of it all, God's Word anchors me so I don't drift away. When I moved back to Dallas after living in Mississippi for sixteen years, I wanted to prepare myself for whatever difficulties might arise. I stenciled this Scripture on my bathroom wall.

My soul finds rest in God alone,
my salvation comes from him.

He alone is my rock and my salvation;
    he is my fortress, I will never be shaken.
(Psalm 62:1–2)

This has become my go-to Scripture when I want to run away. These words speak life to me. They strengthen my resolve and keep me persevering when I'd rather pull the covers over my head and shut out the world. Instead, I run to my Father, my Friend, who waits for me.

Many Christians carry around misconceptions about knowledge. Here's an example. A comment made to me frequently after speaking engagements goes something like this, "You'll be the one thrown into prison for your faith because you know the Bible." I cannot tell you how many people have said this to me. At first, puzzled by these comments, I detected their own fear about knowing too much of God's Word—terrible things might happen to them. Could you compare that to saying, "Because you wear your seat belt, you'll be the one in the car accident"? Wearing a seat belt does not destine me for a car accident, but if I'm in one, I will be prepared. Just because I have portions of God's Word memorized does not make me a candidate for religious imprisonment.

Some people fear too much knowledge, some revere knowledge unduly, others dismiss knowledge as inconsequential. Many discount knowledge because a knowledgeable person disappointed them greatly. When we hear of a pastor or Bible teacher living an immoral life we ask, "What did knowledge do for him?" We conclude that knowing the Bible didn't help that person. Jesus contrasted the wise man and the fool in the Sermon on the Mount. The wise man was the one who heard God's Word and put it into practice. The fool was the one who heard God's Word but did not put it into practice. Both had knowledge. Our growth and maturity depend on our knowledge *and* what we do with that knowledge.

What does it mean to love God with all of our minds? It means, in part, pursuing with our minds the one true God, making Him first over all other intellectual preoccupations. It means choosing to align our minds with His. Memorizing passages helps us do this because we trade our thoughts for God's. We chase after truth, God's truth. We embrace the God of the Bible rather than the god in our own minds. We make a conscious choice to delight in knowing God. We confirm our love for God each day when we persist in the search for true knowledge. We say to God, "I want to know You more so I can love You more."

Memorizing Scripture holds our minds captive so we can focus on God and His thoughts. It disciplines our minds to learn things we want to know. Unexpectedly, I learned many things I didn't want to know. When we memorize books, we inevitably memorize portions we would not otherwise have chosen to memorize, and in so doing our picture of God expands. God takes our concept of Him, pushes out the boundaries we have installed, and shows us wondrous things about Himself. Second Peter is one such example. Chapters 1 and 3 feed the mind with delicious truth. Sandwiched between them is chapter 2, definitely not one we would choose to memorize. It showcases false teachers, their evil deeds, and impending judgment. In that chapter God reveals His no-nonsense attitude toward those who lead others astray. In memorizing chapter 2, our picture of God expands from all-loving and all-merciful to a God of wrath and retributive justice. Whoa! We don't like that picture. I know that I am guilty of creating the god I want and guarding that concept. Memorizing 2 Peter chapter 2 reveals God for who He really is and not just who I want Him to be. My picture of God grows correctly. Memorizing books and passages grounds me in truth that I might otherwise avoid or ignore. The totality of Scripture builds an accurate view of God. This has been huge in my life—beyond estimation. I want to love the God who exists and not the god I imagine.

In one of my seminary classes, Reading Scripture to Change Lives, we memorized a short passage, then presented it to the class, Bible-in-hand, as if reading the text. One day the professor, Dr. Reg Grant, assigned a reading from the Psalms. He instructed us, "Don't choose a psalm everyone loves. Pick one that no one would want to memorize." This task intrigued me, and I dived into it. I settled on Psalm 79. It was perfect—with blood in the streets, birds eating the dead, and an angry, jealous God—yikes! In brief, the psalmist cries out to God in desperation because Jerusalem has been left destitute after the invasion of Babylon and God's people are suffering the grave consequences of their disobedience. The nations mock, "Where is their God?"

Memorizing this psalm sent chills up my spine as the raw emotion pulled me in. Meditating on it took me deep into their anguish, and I entered their struggle. God's redeemed people now suffer after years of disobedience and God's warnings spoken to deaf ears. The psalmist asks for vengeance toward their enemies and deliverance of God's people for the sake of His name. I saw the parallels for the family of God today. We too suffer for our own poor choices and for ignoring God's admonitions. We live in a culture that mocks our God and ridicules His people, the church—much of their scorn deserved and understandable. God assures me through this psalm that He will deal with His enemies in due time and He will deliver the church for the sake of His name and reputation. Strange as it seems, even to me, I've grown to love this psalm. Though I normally would be repulsed by such graphic detail, memorizing and meditating on it pulled back the curtain into the Israelites' desperate lives and I saw myself and my God.

We shouldn't avoid memorizing passages that make us shudder and squirm. They instill a healthy fear in us. My friend Tammy Fabian memorized the book of Hosea, all fourteen chapters, and most of it poetry. I envy the depth she received from that portion of Scripture, even though I didn't choose to memorize it myself. All Scripture is God-breathed, and no portion is irrelevant.

The nicely packaged box that once depicted my God has bulged open, with paper torn, and ribbons hanging. Years ago this would have made me uncomfortable. I wanted a god I could contain in my own mind. No longer. I'm now drawn to His inexhaustible nature, His inexplicable beauty. Mystery does not drive me away. Part of His majesty is in His mystery, and I welcome the intrusion into my meager understanding.

Moses writes, "The secret things belong to the Lord our God, but the things revealed belong to us and to our children forever, that we may follow all the words of this law" (Deuteronomy 29:29). God has not chosen to tell us everything. He is a God beyond human comprehension. Therefore, that's not the goal. The things revealed belong to us, His people, so that we may follow what we've been told. Because of this we shouldn't ignore portions of God's Word that we don't like or that seem difficult. Each book and passage has value and purpose because together they add to the picture of who God is and how He deals with humankind. We live in the light of what we know and believe.

As I continued to immerse myself in God's Word, the bond between me and my heavenly Father grew stronger than I would ever have imagined. Desiring to please Him kept me on the path of obedience, which in turn brought me nearer to His heart. My time in His Word sweetened each day, and the Scriptures I had memorized constantly affirmed me as I reviewed one book every day throughout the day.

A new year arrived. Looking for a fresh opportunity, I decided to take on the book of Hebrews. This unique book connects the Old Testament temple, sacrifices, and priests with their fulfillment in Jesus Christ. I wanted to know and understand these truths more fully. I figured that if I took a chapter a month I could finish in a year. No, wait, with thirteen chapters I would have to squeeze the one in somewhere in order to finish in a year. I began January 1, eager and ready to learn. The message of Hebrews elevates Jesus and the role He came to fulfill. He is

- much superior to the angels,
- worthy of greater honor than Moses,
- a merciful and faithful High Priest,
- a better sacrifice than bulls and goats.

Memorizing the book put me in continual awe of my Savior and all He had done for me. Little did I know that sorrow waited around the corner to ravage my heart and shatter my hope.

My father, who had experienced four heart attacks and

then cancer, died on July 7. Knowing for months that cancer would overcome him, I made two trips to my parents' home in Orlando to plead with him to consider Jesus. Everyone I could possibly think of prayed for my dad, including our two children, ages eight and eleven at the time. But he did not believe that Jesus was the only way to God, and no amount of convincing would change his heart. And so he died—without hope and without Christ.

When the call came that day, we huddled together as a family. My children looked at me with inconsolable faces and said, "What are we going to do?" I remember the words that came out of my mouth: "We're going to trust God. He will get us through this."

An hour later my mother phoned to ask if I would speak at the funeral. I froze. Not that I was unwilling, but what would I say? What could I say? I saw no bright side to this tragedy, no happy ending, no future reunion. It was over. I couldn't get up there and quote a few Bible verses and pretend everything would turn out well. *Oh God, I can't do this!* But I knew I had to. My mother had just lost a husband of forty-five years. My children had lost their "Pop." There would be other family members there as well as my father's coworkers and golfing buddies. So I would trust God, and He would be with me.

The most difficult assignment of my life had just been handed to me. I called my closest friends to pray for me, hold me up, and protect me from despair. I needed help in writing and delivering a tribute to my father.

We got our things together and packed the car. An hour before we left, my friend Melissa dropped by and said, "I thought this might be helpful," as she handed me Dennis Rainey's book *The Tribute* (Thomas Nelson), a book about writing a tribute to parents. No doubt that gift was from the hand of God.

During the twelve-hour drive, I read the book, much of the time by flashlight, and wrote a tribute to my father. From a human perspective, I was fragile and vulnerable, but in the truest sense, God was my refuge and strength. His presence surrounded me and gave me the courage to face the task, even though my heart was breaking. I clung to His words as if they were my very life. And when the time came for me to speak, "God's grace and peace were mine in abundance."

When I returned home to Hattiesburg, my friends showered me with love and support. The ever-present truths of Hebrews kept me clinging to God. After spending months in Hebrews, meditating on all that Jesus did to give me access to the Holy of Holies, the very throne room of God, I had no reason to stand afar in the outer court. I came boldly and often to His throne of grace and He always met me there.

Several weeks later, on a Sunday night in church after we had sung praises to God, a visiting evangelist got up to speak. He said, "Tonight I'm going to tell you the truth about hell." Caught totally off guard, sitting in the second row, I felt conspicuous and trapped. As I moved closer to Ethan, he put his arm around me, both of us dreading the sermon. By the end of the service, distraught and beaten down, we made a beeline for the exit and drove home in silence.

The next morning during my prayer time, I cried out in desperation. "God, I can't cry myself to sleep every night because my father is heading for a place of torment. I know too much to pretend it isn't true, and I don't know how to live with this." And, momentarily in my heart, I doubted that even God's Word had an answer for this.

Later on that day, while folding laundry, I was reviewing the book of Philippians from memory, which I did every Monday. When I got to the part in chapter 3 that says, "I want to know Christ and the power of his resurrection and the fellowship of sharing in his sufferings," my concentration broke, interrupted with a new thought. "There's your answer. Now you do know, in small measure, the suffering of God's Son. You know the pain caused by one you love who rejects the truth. You know the pain caused by sin, the pain caused by pride and indifference. Now you're experiencing the fellowship of His suffering."

Once again God's Word provided answers, though not easy ones. It truly is everything I need for life and godliness.

I share this pain with you because I am not unique. God did not exempt any of us from suffering. We carry emotional scars from ended relationships, financial reversals, tragedies and betrayals, serious or chronic illnesses, and private wounds that cannot be shared with anyone. We will all be tested through trials. Peter tells us it's God's way of proving that our faith is genuine. When things don't go our way, will we still believe? Will we still obey? Will we continue to trust God even if He says no to our prayers—or doesn't answer at all?

Adversity sprinkles every life; no family goes untouched. Heartache and struggle persist in every home. When hardship knocks at your door, how will you deal with it? Will you retreat into depression? Will you lash out at your spouse? At your kids? At God? What will you tell your children when life is cruel and unfair? When God could have intervened but didn't? They learn to deal with life's disappointments by watching you. If you don't trust God, will they?

God intended His Word to anchor us in the storms of

life. Within the pages of His Book, He builds, precept upon precept, a picture of the One we can trust. This perfectly righteous God, holy in all His ways, knows all things and sees the beginning and the end and whatever lies in between. His power and authority orchestrate all events and work out everything in conformity with the purpose of His will. He is the ultimate Ruler over all nations and is sovereign in the affairs of humankind.

Do I understand all of this? No, but I accept it, nonetheless. And most beneficial from my human perspective, this Father invited me into His family, redeemed me at great cost, and cares about my welfare. This is the God I have read about and have come to know, and so I trust Him.

This trust is no doubt the by-product of God's Word sown in my life. Memorizing Scripture doesn't make me trust God, but it consistently gives me a picture of a trustworthy God. My heartache over my father's lost condition remains with me, although I've become more numb over time. Without God's Word to sustain me, I can only imagine where I would be—either in denial or despair. My father's situation goes beyond my human capacity to deal with or resolve, either emotionally or providentially. So I have left the matter with God, and I choose to trust Him. He doesn't have to report to me. He owes me no explanation. His Word says that one day all tears and sorrow will cease. This promise endures even in the pain. I choose to believe it, and until then I'll keep trusting God to be my refuge from a situation I cannot change.

Just as there is a definite link between knowing God and knowing His Word, so there is an inseparable connection between knowing God's Word and trusting Him. As God communicates truth in His Word, I have something to put my trust in. It's a progressive learning experience—the more I trust God for things He has made known in His Word, the more I am able to trust Him for the mysteries He has not made known. Trust is a choice based on knowledge.

> O send out Your light and Your truth, let them lead me;
> Let them bring me to Your holy hill
> And to Your dwelling places.
> Then I will go to the altar of God,
> To God my exceeding joy;
> And upon the lyre I shall praise You, O God, my God.
> (Psalm 43:3–4 NASB)

5>>
YOUR TURN:
CAPTURE MOMENTS

YOUR NEXT OPPORTUNITY AWAITS. You breezed right through Psalm 1, so we're moving to a bigger challenge—the book of Titus, a letter rich in doctrine for practical living. Before I memorized this book, I could not have given you even a brief summary of it, even though I'd read it countless times. Might this also be true for you, that you've read Titus many times but couldn't state the central message of the book? I guarantee that after memorizing Titus, or any other book, you will never forget the content, even if you forget the word-for-word text. I treasure the books I've learned this way because I gained confidence in differentiating the Bible's content book by book.

Titus has forty-six verses in three chapters. Get ready to be amazed at how much you can learn from one small book. Train yourself to look for snippets of time in your day. If you will include Scripture memory as part of your morning routine, it will more likely become a permanent part of your life. It's also an energizing way to start your day that will not take any extra time. If you're in the habit of watching TV or listening to the radio while getting ready in the morning, make the great exchange—trade in man's words for God's.

Before you begin, you will need to get Titus into a form you can take with you. Write out Titus chapter 1 on the same index-card spiral that contains Psalm 1. Or print Titus from your computer, or set your Bible app to Titus on your phone or notebook or tablet. Bookmark it. I enjoy writing out the chapter because it motivates me to see ahead of time what I will be learning. I will walk you through the first ten days.

Day 1

— ◆ —

TITUS 1 : 1

Paul, a servant of God and an apostle of Jesus Christ for the faith of God's elect and the knowledge of the truth that leads to godliness—

◆ Say the first verse out loud, again and again.

◆ Move segment by segment until you think you have it—about ten or fifteen times.

◆ This one verse will take approximately eight seconds to review.

◆ Look at it again while making breakfast. The toaster takes longer than reciting this verse.

◆ Share it with your spouse or your kids, even if the child is only two years old. They'll love it!

◆ Take your verses with you in the car on the way to work or school.

◆ Consider what the verse says. Ask yourself questions.

◆ Who? Paul. How does he describe himself? A servant of God and an apostle of Jesus Christ.

◆ Why is he writing? For the faith of God's elect and the knowledge of the truth.

◆ Where does the knowledge of the truth lead? It leads to godliness.

◆ Is this what you want? Yes. Then go after truth. That's why we're doing this.

◆ This verse contains so much to meditate on. Think about it. Pray about it. Let it come alive in you.

◆ Review this one verse throughout your day, fifteen to twenty times. You are training yourself to capture moments for God's Word.

Day 2

— ◆ —

TITUS 1 : 2

a faith and knowledge resting on the hope
of eternal life which God, who does not lie,
promised before the beginning of time,

◆ Begin reviewing verse I first thing in the morning. See if you remember it from yesterday.

◆ Move on to verse 2. Say verses I and 2 out loud, line by line, until you have them by heart.

◆ It doesn't matter if this takes ten or fifteen times. This is normal.

◆ Throughout your day focus on these two verses.

◆ Think about what verse 2 says. Chew on it in your mind.

◆ Ask questions: who, what, where, when, why, and how.

◆ Where is my faith resting? On the hope of eternal life.

◆ Who promised this? God. When? Before the beginning of time.

◆ What attribute of God is mentioned? He does not lie. Wow!

◆ How sure is your faith? As sure as God Himself.

◆ Think about this all day long. Let the richness of this truth consume your thoughts.

◆ Send out a tweet and share these two verses. Better make that two tweets because of character limits.

Day 3

— ◆ —

TITUS 1 : 3

and at his appointed season he brought his word
to light through the preaching entrusted
to me by the command of God our Savior,

◆ Review verses 1 and 2 as soon as you get up. Try to do this without looking, and see if you have it.

◆ Move on to verse 3. Take it line by line. Say it with the other two verses.

◆ Can you see that even now, at God's appointed season, He is bringing His Word to light for you through Paul's teaching in the book of Titus? Thank God for all you are learning.

◆ Look for opportunities to squeeze in twenty-five seconds for verses 1 through 3. Noon, mid-afternoon, dinnertime.

◆ Come back to God's Word at the end of the day. Thank God for this incredible experience.

◆ Don't forget to review Psalm 1 on your designated day each week.

Day 4

— ◆ —

TITUS 1 : 4

To Titus, my true son in our common faith:
Grace and peace from God the Father and Christ Jesus our
Savior.

◆ As soon as you wake up, direct your thoughts toward God's Word. Review your three verses.

◆ Start today's verse. Break it down phrase by phrase. Say all four verses together.

◆ Identify times in your day when your hands are busy but your mind is free: as you fold laundry, vacuum the house, boil water, wait on hold, wait in traffic.

◆ Push the mute button on the remote during commercials. You know how long commercials are.

◆ Don't let your mind wander into Never-never-land. Seize those idle moments for God's Word.

◆ Are you working out at the gym or at home? Exercise your mind at the same time.

◆ Conclude your day by meditating on God's Word. How blessed you will be!

Day 5

— ◆ —

TITUS 1 : 5

The reason I left you in Crete was
that you might straighten out what was left unfinished
and appoint elders in every town, as I directed you.

◆ Begin your day focused on God's Word. Review your previous verses.

◆ Add today's verse. You will be up to forty-five seconds for all five verses.

◆ Paul now gives his purpose for writing this letter. Ask God to give you insights.

◆ Keep your verses in front of you while you get ready for the day. Carry your verses wherever you go.

◆ Use driving time to learn today's verse. Red lights are perfect for checking yourself.

◆ Whatever you're doing, welcome God's Word into your day.

◆ While you're cooking supper and cleaning up, steer your mind back to God's Word.

◆ Can you sense God disciplining your mind to focus on Him?

◆ Give your last few minutes before bed to think about your verses in Titus.

Day 6

TITUS 1:6

An elder must be blameless, the husband of but one wife, a man whose children believe and are not open to the charge of being wild and disobedient.

◆ You are establishing a habit of giving your first thoughts of the day to God.

◆ Don't miss even one day. It makes such a difference in your outlook.

◆ Paul now gives Titus qualifications for elders, leaders of the church.

◆ Review your previous verses and then add today's verse.

◆ As you go about your day, meditate on what you have learned so far.

◆ Are you running errands today? Take your verses with you.

◆ Review while you're waiting at the Starbucks drive-thru, the post office, the DMV.

◆ When your mind gets tired, just read the verses. You are still reinforcing the words.

Day 7

—— ◆ ——

TITUS 1 : 7

Since an overseer is entrusted with God's work,
he must be blameless—not overbearing, not
quick-tempered, not given to drunkenness,
not violent, not pursuing dishonest gain.

◆ Even if you're not a morning person, memorizing God's Word makes getting up more pleasant.

◆ Go over your verses in the shower. See if you're on target so far.

◆ Add today's verse. Learn it phrase by phrase or line by line.

◆ Think about why God included each of these qualifications for leadership in the church. The answer is in the word *since*. Have you also been entrusted with God's work? Think about it.

◆ Share what you're learning with your children. They need to know these things, and it will only take a minute or two. How will they know unless you tell them? Don't count on someone else.

◆ What are you doing today that will let you fit in a minute to practice? Are you sweeping the front porch, raking leaves, doing some gardening, mowing the lawn, walking the dog?

Day 8

—— ◆ ——

TITUS 1 :8

Rather he must be hospitable, one who loves what is good,
who is self-controlled, upright, holy and disciplined.

◆ It's a new day with a new verse. Review your other verses first, and then tackle the new one.

◆ Are the qualities listed only for elders, or does God want each of us to attain to these standards?

◆ Are you pursuing these? Ask God to build them into your life.

◆ Who doesn't need the character described here? What would it look like for you to love what is good?

◆ Meditate on this list throughout your day. Let it roll over and over in your mind.

◆ Don't miss what God is saying to you. Make each line a prayer.

◆ By working on these verses throughout your day, you are training and disciplining your mind.

Day 9

— ◆ —

TITUS 1:9

*He must hold firmly to the trustworthy message
as it has been taught, so that he can encourage others
by sound doctrine and refute those who oppose it.*

◆ As soon as you open your eyes for the new day, let your thoughts gravitate to God's Word.

◆ Your review of verses 1–8 will take about one minute.

◆ Start your new verse. Combine it with your previous verses.

◆ What is the message here? Ask yourself: What must he do, and why? Is this also for you?

◆ By memorizing God's Word you are becoming familiar with God's message so that you can encourage others by sound doctrine. And you can defend truth to those who are antagonistic.

◆ Grab those spare moments between tasks. What better way to maximize your time?

◆ Bring your day to a close by reviewing and meditating on what God says in Titus.

Day 10
— ◆ —

TITUS 1 : 1 0

For there are many rebellious people, mere talkers and deceivers, especially those of the circumcision group.

◆ Maintain the discipline of putting God's Word first in your day. Review what you have learned so far.

◆ If you have trouble recalling the nine verses, you probably have not reviewed them enough times. A good goal is fifteen to twenty times in a day. Each person needs to find a personal rhythm.

◆ Move on when you are ready. Today's verse gives the reason for verse 9.

◆ Do we find people like this today? Yes, and we're all vulnerable to their influence.

◆ As you repeat this verse, cry out to God, asking Him to keep you from becoming one of them.

◆ Share your progress with someone who would be edified. Ask that person to check up on you later.

◆ Give the final moments of your day to God. Rehearse His Word as you drift off to sleep.

◆ If you need a break tomorrow in order to catch up, then do so. But be careful that your flexibility doesn't reduce your habit-forming discipline. Too many days off take you backward. On the other hand, falling behind is also deflating and makes you tempted to quit. Press on!

Day 11

◆

TITUS 1:11

They must be silenced, because they are ruining whole households by teaching things they ought not to teach— and that for the sake of dishonest gain.

Day 12

◆

TITUS 1:12

Even one of their own prophets has said, "Cretans are always liars, evil brutes, lazy gluttons."

Day 13

◆

TITUS 1:13

This testimony is true. Therefore, rebuke them sharply, so that they will be sound in the faith

Day 14

◆

TITUS 1:14

and will pay no attention to Jewish myths or to the commands of those who reject the truth.

Day 15

TITUS 1:15

To the pure, all things are pure, but to those who
are corrupted and do not believe, nothing is pure.
In fact, both their minds and consciences are corrupted.

Day 16

TITUS 1:16

They claim to know God, but by their actions
they deny him. They are detestable, disobedient
and unfit for doing anything good.

You made it. You finished an entire chapter. Wow! Don't you feel energized? Something significant took place in your life. You trained yourself to give your free thoughts to God instead of to daydreaming. You redeemed the time that might have been wasted. Now you're planted by streams of water and drinking deeply. I'm so proud of you. Discipline comes at a price, but, oh the rewards!

A FEW TIPS

- Before you begin Titus chapter 2, take a few days just for review of chapter 1. You want to solidify this chapter in your mind before you move on. The entire chapter will take approximately two minutes to review. By now you're finding two-minute pockets in your day. In chapter 7 we will go through Titus chapters 2 and 3.
- While reviewing chapter 1, ask yourself, *How does God*

want me to apply these truths in my life? Listen, and let God show you. Ask Him to keep His words alive in your heart and to transform you into "one who loves what is good."

● Take this review time to remind yourself of anything that was confusing or unclear. Look up in a good commentary any questions that linger. For example, verse 12 quotes some prophet proclaiming that Cretans are liars, brutes, and gluttons. What's that all about? Paul is quoting the Cretan prophet Epimenides. It helps to know the background. There are so many interesting things to learn.

You will find that the discipline of memorizing Scripture becomes more automatic the more you do it. Each time you capture idle moments for God's Word, you condition yourself to produce self-governing habits. And you will attain your ultimate goal of keeping your focus on God throughout your day, in the midst of life's other demands.

All people can find windows of time in their routine if they look for them. Years ago I took my two teenagers to the orthodontist once a month for four years, two years each. Instead of sitting in the waiting room listening to secular music and reading tacky magazines, I often waited outside in my car, going over my verses. You can cover a lot of territory in thirty to forty-five minutes. This one example worked for me. It wouldn't work with a three-year-old in the car. You will find your own segments of time as you look for them.

Recently while speaking at a women's conference, a woman shared her situation with me during lunch. She is a nurse who takes care of bedridden patients in their homes. Her current patient sleeps most of the day because of her medication. After hearing my tips on capturing moments throughout the day, she told me she wastes precious hours doing Sudoku puzzles, surfing the Internet, and reading trivial publications. She said she couldn't wait to get back to work and use that time for memorizing God's Word instead.

The following email was included in my first book. Karen wrote me several months after one of my speaking engagements:

Hi, Janet!

I've been wanting to let you know how your words have borne fruit in my life. I am very reluctant to jump into people's "programs," as I often experience more frustration than progress, so I really only went to your seminar because my friend Renee wanted to attend! (True confessions) And to underscore that, I really only began to memorize the Scripture because Renee said, "Let's both do Psalm 119!"

I enjoyed what you shared and agreed that Scripture memory is important, but it was hearing you recite it that made me want to do it, because it was then that I knew the Scripture was not just in your head but in your heart. However, I still needed Renee's push to get started.

Anyway, I have wanted to let you know that simply doing a verse a day and doing whole portions of Scripture have been wonderfully used in my life. A couple of years ago I began weightlifting and experienced lots of physical benefits, and I compare what is happening in my mind and heart to that. It's sort of like taking vitamins for my soul. Anyway, I wanted to encourage you, as this has been the most significant "power surge" I have experienced since I first became a believer!

In Christ, Karen Burroughs

That email was sent to me more than ten years ago. I recently contacted Karen and asked her to follow up on what years of memorizing have meant to her long-term.

Hi, Janet,

Fourteen years ago I reluctantly agreed to memorize Psalm 119 with a friend. And now, years later, with many books of Scripture memorized, I'm so thankful that I took the challenge! This relationship of hiding His Word in my heart has been significant beyond words and life-changing for me! I feel amazed, grateful, and content. I am amazed at how meditating and pondering on a passage until it is embedded in my memory has strengthened my daily experience of walking in faith. God's Word is alive and speaking to me at every turn.

I am grateful for the strength and courage that blossomed in the face of my husband's leukemia diagnosis. Our lives were turned upside down and slammed by the stormy waves of treatments and health issues, but my heart and soul were anchored in God's Word. And as I look to the future, even though the world is brimming with chaos and confusion, I sense an ever-growing contentment with His will for me—delighting to embrace the circumstances that come my way. I can't thank you enough for challenging me to dig deeper and plant His Word in the innermost recesses of my soul. I am indeed reaping a rich harvest.

Karen

What a beautiful testimony! Karen exemplifies one who meditates on God's Word every day, allowing it to impact every aspect of her life. I wanted you to see that I'm not the only person memorizing books and passages. There's an army out there, growing bigger and stronger every day.

Ask yourself, how would my life be different if I made God's Word my daily delight? If throughout my day, God's Word rolled around in my head, if I made it a habit of thinking through the implications of a passage instead of just reading it?

Time, a precious commodity, allots each of us twenty-four hours a day. I'm not by nature an efficient time manager, but I've learned to utilize little moments here and there for God's Word. Although two-minute slots may seem insignificant, they add up to an enormous amount over a twenty-year period. I've now memorized fifteen books and many other passages, in total more than 140 chapters of the Bible. I share that as proof that great progress comes a few minutes at a time.

Oh, how I love your law!
I meditate on it all day long. (Psalm 119:97)

6»
THE BENEFITS TO
OUR SANCTIFICATION

OUR SON AUSTIN CAME INTO the world with one foot bent sideways. We sought out a pediatric orthopedist who explained to us that his completely normal foot became cramped in the womb and then continued to grow in the wrong direction.

As expected, this doctor did not ask for our suggestions or ideas for Austin's treatment; he had his own procedure. Austin would need to wear orthopedic shoes that would hold both feet together with an eight-inch metal brace. The doctor assured us that if we followed his instructions precisely, Austin would have a perfect foot in about a year, with no lasting effects. If we didn't follow his orders, Austin would be impaired for the rest of his life. Given these two outcomes, we understood our responsibility.

The instructions were simple: Keep the shoes on at all times, except while bathing, and buy new shoes every four or five weeks. That didn't sound too complicated. We left the doctor's office with our six-week-old baby boy and his tiny new shoes. So relieved at the good news, we determined to be faithful to the guidelines, wanting nothing less than a perfect foot for our son.

Before we even pulled into our driveway, Austin began to cry. He did not like those new shoes. With his feet bound together, he couldn't move one without the other. He cried, he screamed, he got mad, he fought and kicked and begged us with his eyes to stop the torture. He didn't understand his new reality or why we allowed this cruelty. We felt sorry for him, but we loved him too much to give in, no matter how much he cried. That first day and night, he wailed constantly until exhaustion overcame him and he fell asleep.

The next day we flew to Florida to visit grandparents. We skipped his bath that morning because we were afraid to take the shoes off and give him momentary freedom, only to take it away and cause the crying all over again. The following day we removed the shoes to bathe him. Poor little guy! He had kicked and fought so much that he had a terrible blister on his heel, already broken, sore and red. It was almost too much for a mother to bear.

I called the doctor in Dallas and asked if we could keep the shoes off until it healed. He said, "Absolutely not. If it hurts him enough, he'll quit kicking." For the next twelve months we rigidly followed the doctor's orders. Austin's foot grew and grew, and he ended up with a perfect pair—now size 13½.

What's the point to this story? Like Austin, every one of us came into the world defective. Genesis 1–2 tells us that God created humans in His own image, but the Fall recorded in Genesis 3 marred the image and tainted the rest of humankind with sin.

God has a plan to redeem humankind through a Savior and restore those He has redeemed back to the original image. God's redemption plan brings about our salvation. God's restoration plan brings about our sanctification. Though not a word used in everyday conversation, *sanctification* is the process whereby we grow into Christlikeness. Through our own striving for holiness and cooperating with the indwelling Holy

Spirit, God sets us apart and transforms us into the likeness of His Son, Jesus, the model of the perfect man.

As should be expected, God, the Master Designer, doesn't ask our advice or weigh our suggestions. He has His own procedure, and He wants us to follow it.

God gave us a Book of instructions and also a resident Helper, His Holy Spirit. As we follow the instructions, with the help of God's indwelling Spirit, He works in us, conforming us to His original design. Ignoring the instructions leads to continued impairment. We may kick and scream and blame God, but He loves us too much to change the instructions. He wants nothing less than perfection for His sons and daughters.

Over three decades of Christian ministry, I've observed that many believers read their Bibles dutifully and listen to sermons attentively, but they remain unclear on how God intends to use His Word to make them more like Jesus.

Jesus prayed for all believers, "Sanctify them by the truth; your word is truth" (John 17:17).

I'm taking you back to 2 Peter for some clarity.

His divine power has given us everything we need for life and godliness through our knowledge of him who called us by his own glory and goodness. Through these he has given us his very great and precious promises so that through them you may participate in the divine nature and escape the corruption in the world caused by evil desires. (2 Peter 1:3–4)

Peter asserts that, through the very great and precious promises of God, believers can participate in the divine nature and escape the corruption in the world caused by evil desires.

In context, this means that the promises God has given us in His Word enable us to grow in godly character (become more like Jesus) and stay above the moral decay in the world. These verses are then followed by a call to grow in virtue (2 Peter 1:5–8).

We know from God's Word that the divine nature dwells in us through the Holy Spirit (1 Corinthians 3:16; 6:19; Galatians 4:6; 1 John 4:13). Peter affirms that God has made provision for our growth in Christlikeness and our moral victory over sin.

God plans to use His Word to mature us. But it's not accomplished just by *knowing* the promises of God, as essential as that is. Knowledge is one part of the equation, but knowledge alone cannot produce Christlikeness. We must follow the instructions God has given us.

Last year, when trying to decide what to memorize next, I returned to words from Jesus. I want to listen to Him so that I can emulate Him. I had already memorized the Sermon on the Mount, so I chose another famous passage, John 13–17, known as the Upper Room Discourse—five chapters devoted to Jesus' final words to His disciples the night before He went to the cross. I divided the passage into twelve segments, making it a one-year project, then recruited my friend Susan Turner to join me. We spent the year pouring over this intimate conversation between God in the flesh and the I-still-don't-get-it disciples.

This was Jesus' last shot to pass on what they would need to know and do after He left. How would they carry on Jesus' mission and make an impact that would spread to the whole world? What instructions did He leave them?

If you love me, you will obey what I command.
(John 14:15)

Whoever has my commands and obeys them, he is the one who loves me. (John 14:21)

Jesus had already clarified the greatest commandment—love God. Now He tells them what love for God looks like.

Love = obedience to God's commands.

So was Jesus teaching this for the disciples' growth and sanctification or as part of His strategy to reach the world? Both. Our growth is inseparably linked to our witness to the world. If we want to jolt our self-absorbed, self-promoting, celebrity-worshiping society into taking notice of our alternative lifestyle, then let them see the followers of Jesus living distinctly different from other people. Let them see the divine nature in us. Let them see Christians escaping the sins the rest of the world succumbs to. That might get their attention.

Can we examine ourselves with a tough question? Does our culture mock and ridicule Christians because of the tenets of our faith or because of the incongruity in our lives? Ouch! Jesus gets a bad rap when His so-called followers don't follow. They don't follow the Book they claim to live by.

So how can we change that? Jesus didn't mention memorizing Scripture, but His emphasis on obeying His commands assumed their familiarity.

What about you and me? Can we live out the doctrines and exhortations of our faith if we don't know them? Can we be sure we will remain on the road-less-traveled in a culture that entices with duct-taped realities? Will we hear the still, small voice of God if we allow endless noise to drown it out?

God's plan for believers involves total dedication to

knowing and following His Word. Memorizing passages helps me accomplish that in my life. Time spent in God's Word gives me a more comprehensive understanding of my faith. Reviewing Scripture periodically throughout each day and night keeps my heart in tune with the Lord and shows me how to live out the gospel—the only hope for the world.

The habit of saying God's Word over and over throughout the day results in more obedience in my life. God's double-edged sword exposes my hidden motives and reveals the wretched nature I've concealed all my life. God pinpoints what He wants to clean up or move out so that I can grow.

One area that needed changing was loving the things of the world, which, in this case, I'm taking literally. I struggle because—I admit it—I love things! I love pretty things. I love useful things. I love expensive things. I love buying things for people. I love buying things for myself. So what's the problem? God's Word tells us:

> Do not love the world or anything in the world. If anyone loves the world, the love of the Father is not in him. For everything in the world—the cravings of sinful man, the lust of his eyes and the boasting of what he has and does—comes not from the Father but from the world. The world and its desires pass away, but the man who does the will of God lives forever. (1 John 2:15–17)

When I began memorizing the book of 1 John, I saw it coming, and I knew I would have to deal with it. I said these words again and again, repeating them to myself and making them a plea to the Lord to change me. God's Word told me that if I loved the world and its things, then I did not love

Him. The truth jabbed me. I found myself sighing, moaning, and shaking my head, "I don't want to love the world!"

I agonized over this area of weakness. Divided affections held me back from being all that God intended. I didn't want to be in bondage to those things that enslave the rest of the world. God's Word spoke truth, and I couldn't rationalize it away. It stirred within me the desire to change. I can honestly say that today I don't love the world or material things the way I used to, though this will probably always be an area of vulnerability for me.

In 2005 Hurricane Katrina pummeled the Gulf Coast. Although New Orleans got most of the press coverage, Mississippi received the direct hit. Living in Hattiesburg at the time, about 70 miles from the coast, we knew for days that a monster was headed our way, and many evacuated voluntarily. I would have been among them, but my *brave* husband decided to ride it out. Our kids, off at college, were safe from harm.

The night before the storm we prepared for the invasion. I looked around the house and asked myself what I needed to protect. I moved our family pictures from one closet to another. Then I surveyed my things. A contented peace came over me when I realized there was nothing here I wasn't willing to lose.

The day of the storm, Ethan and I sat in a windowless bathroom under the stairs—for five hours. Tornado winds caused by the hurricane swirled through our neighborhood. The walls shook, trees fell on the house, and windows shattered. In the midst of it all, I thought about how God had done an incredible work in me through the years. Things I once treasured had lost their grip on me.

Although we sustained damage to both our home and

office, the cleanup was more inconvenience than personal loss. Months later we put together a five-picture collage that now hangs in our new office. Our kids think it's weird that we memorialized our battered house and debris-filled yard, but for me it represents much more—an internal victory that no storm could destroy.

Memorizing passages hasn't removed temptation from my life, but when I'm seduced by the world and the things it promises, I know where to go for relief. I don't have to look up the words; they're stored in my mind, ready to be retrieved.

One summer a time of waiting on God dissolved into frustration. Desiring to breathe fresh air into my stale perspective, I looked for something to memorize. I chose Isaiah 55, which includes these words:

> "For my thoughts are not your thoughts,
>   neither are your ways my ways," declares the Lord.
> "As the heavens are higher than the earth,
>   so are my ways higher than your ways
>   and my thoughts than your thoughts."
> (Isaiah 55:8–9)

These words, already familiar to me, took on new life as I memorized them. Saying them over and over, I scrutinized the meaning.

I saw myself as a sniveling child trying to manipulate a wavering parent. I had reduced God to human attributes—an imperfect father, too tired, indecisive, or locked in a schedule jam. I don't know why God put my request on hold; He never told me. But He spoke through Isaiah, "My way is best. I've thought it out, and I know what I'm doing."

God's thoughts and ways differ from mine. They so far exceed my feeble attempts that I can't even fathom the distance. The truth humbled me, and I surrendered.

You might be asking, "Does hearing from God require memorizing?" No, but listening to God often requires deep contemplation, and memorizing lays the groundwork for that.

Isaiah 55, a never-ending feast for the soul, continues with these words:

> "As the rain and the snow
>   come down from heaven,
> and do not return to it
>   without watering the earth
> and making it bud and flourish,
>   so that it yields seed for the sower and bread for the
>   eater,
> so is my word that goes out from my mouth:
>   It will not return to me empty,
> but will accomplish what I desire
>   and achieve the purpose for which I sent it."
> (Isaiah 55:10–11)

God compares His Word to the rain and the snow that water the earth and cause life and growth.

I'd always loved these verses, but I'd never connected them to the two preceding verses about God's thoughts and ways. After saying the verses together dozens of times, a light went on. How is God's Word like the rain and the snow that produce growth? God's Word contains God's thoughts and God's ways, and this is what brings forth growth in us. When we get into God's Word, it becomes our pipeline to God's way of thinking and doing things.

As I stay in God's Word, abide in God's Word, drink in God's Word, it will do its work in me, the work it was sent to do. It will accomplish God's desire and achieve His purpose, which is to cause growth in me by bringing my thoughts and my ways into alignment with His.

Isaiah 55 invites the thirsty to come and drink freely and then promises delight for the soul. It reassures me that God's Word in me will not return void. It will bring forth life and growth—my sanctification.

The psalmist testifies to the value of meditating on God's Word.

> How can a young man keep his way pure?
>> By living according to your word.
> I seek you with all my heart;
>> do not let me stray from your commands.
> I have hidden your word in my heart
>> that I might not sin against you.
> Praise be to you, O Lord;
>> teach me your decrees.
> With my lips I recount
>> all the laws that come from your mouth.
> I rejoice in following your statutes
>> as one rejoices in great riches.
> I meditate on your precepts
>> and consider your ways.
> I delight in your decrees;
>> I will not neglect your word. (Psalm 119:9–16)

My own experience parallels the psalmist's sentiments. When I seek God with all my heart, keep His words on my lips, and meditate on His precepts, my heart delights in Him and I have no desire to stray.

What about the charge that knowledge puffs up and inflates the ego? I've heard that one a million times. Actually, knowledge without obedience makes one prideful, but true experiential knowledge makes one humble. When Isaiah saw a vision of God seated on His throne, high and exalted, he saw himself for what he really was: unworthy and unclean (Isaiah 6:1–5). When the apostle Peter realized that Jesus was the Christ, he said, "Go away from me, Lord; I am a sinful man!" (Luke 5:8). As we submit to God in obedience to His Word, we will keep the right perspective on ourselves.

Our actions will always follow our beliefs. We live out each day what we truly believe. As God's Word cements truth into our hearts and minds, it results in a change in lifestyle, a change that reflects God's values over our own. Obedience remains the true test of genuine faith.

But something within us resists obedience. Can you identify with the well-known hymn by Robert Robinson (1735–90), "Come, Thou Fount of Every Blessing"?

> Prone to wander, Lord, I feel it,
> Prone to leave the God I love;
> Here's my heart, O take and seal it;
> Seal it for thy courts above.

Robinson recognized his human frailties, his proclivity to stray from the truth. And he cited the root of his problem, his deceptive heart. Thus, he asked God to take his heart and seal it so that it would be useful for God's kingdom only. Did he mean seal his heart so that nothing else could penetrate it, or was he asking God to put His insignia on it so that God claims it as belonging to Him? I don't know. I do know that without intentionality in my routine, I easily float downstream and end up where I don't want to be. Regular reminders and promptings tether me to the truth so I don't drift away.

Nestled among other trinkets from my travels, a unique ship illustrates God's handiwork. Having traveled to Russia eight times, I've become familiar with many types of crafts and handmade souvenirs found in the outdoor markets. Far exceeding the others, the ship in the bottle fascinates me. There's nothing special about the bottle itself; the intrigue lies in the meticulous detail seen through the glass. Like me, many of the uninformed wonder, "How do they get the ship into the bottle through the narrow neck?" The answer is, they don't. They build it from the inside!

Four things are necessary: a clear bottle, a skilled craftsman, a long stick-like tool, and a model to work from. The craftsman uses his tool and carefully constructs the ship with miniature pieces, working toward an exact replica of the model. These ships can't be mass-produced; they have to be done one at a time.

This compares to our sanctification. We are the glass bottle. The craftsman is the Holy Spirit. His tool is the Word of God, and the model is Jesus. The emerging masterpiece causes others to see Jesus in our lives and wonder how He got inside.

7»
YOUR TURN: SOAK IT IN

AN INTERNET SEARCH FOR the perfect cup of tea produced connoisseurs from all over the globe eager to share their pointers. I only wanted to spend a minute, not a fortnight. I learned that the art of making tea ranges from mechanics to snobbery ("Never use tea bags!"). Tea lovers employ a range of techniques but all have the same objective: to steep the tea until it permeates every part of the water.

Memorizing Scripture and meditating on it compare to steeping tea. The how-to of memorizing really doesn't matter. However you choose to memorize, let it soak in. Let the Word of God saturate every part of you, and then take pleasure in the result.

One summer I received a most encouraging letter. An abbreviated version follows:

> Dear Janet,
>
>   About three years ago I really began to have a desire to memorize Scripture. I had set monthly and yearly goals, albeit small ones, and set out to learn verses at random. Though God blessed me in pressing some special verses on my heart, I wasn't satisfied with my attempts at hiding His Word in my heart. Time passed, and this spring you came to speak to the ladies at our church. With eagerness I attended. Your love for Christ and His Word radiated from you. You weren't proud or

legalistic. You were just in love with God and enthusiastic to encourage others to get to know God.

Here sits an inspired listener. I am so excited about God and His Word. He has enabled me to memorize 2 Peter and the first chapter of Colossians. Rather than worrying or speculating about some gossip I may have heard, I review Scripture. When my quiet husband enjoys silence on a car ride, I enjoy reviewing Scripture. When I wake up and can't sleep, I go over those verses again. As God provides opportunities, I share with others how exciting it's been to get to know Him.

God's Word must permeate every aspect of our lives. God can, indeed will, change our lives as we get to know Him. Sometimes I cry when I realize how precious God has been to me. What a joy that He allows us to get just a glimpse of who He is. Janet, thank you for pointing me in the right direction. God has used your willingness to share to bring me to new levels of knowing God. May God bless your ministry and lead many others to desire and to discipline themselves to know Him.

In Christ,
Cindy

In a few months' time, Cindy memorized one book and started another. She found joy not in the accomplishment but in the resulting changes in her relationship with God, reaching new levels of knowing Him. As she closes her letter, she expresses hope that many others will desire and discipline themselves to know God. Cindy aptly summarizes what it takes—desire and discipline. I also believe that many would discipline themselves if only they had the desire.

The annual Bible Girls Retreat, hosted by my friend Richie Malone, takes place at her secluded lodge in Colorado.

For five wintery days, ten friends get away, listen to teaching from God's Word, and discuss by the fire. To my great delight, I've been their teacher for the past six years. We cook simple meals, share honest fellowship around the table, and support each other in the muck of life. Since our relationships have gone deeper through the years, greater trust allows more freedom to call each other out.

One year, on our final night, one of the women said to me, "I wish I had your discipline." Having heard that comment so many times, I usually shrug my shoulders, shake my head, and sigh at their predicament. This time, out of love and boldness, I took a different approach. I said, "What if I said to you, 'You have so much discipline. It's just incredible how you find time every single day to eat breakfast, lunch, and dinner; you hardly ever miss. You are so disciplined.' You would then say to me, 'It's not discipline—I'm hungry.' Now, I will say to you, 'Your problem is not lack of discipline. Your problem is that you're not hungry.'"

Sometimes the truth stings, but let's not confuse a lack of discipline with a lack of desire. People discipline themselves when they perceive the outcome to far exceed the effort. You turn on the news and watch people camping out at stores for days in order to buy the newest iPhone, $100 wedding dresses, or playoff tickets. When interviewed, their enthusiasm outweighs any sleep deprivation or inconvenience. They don't think of it as discipline; they consider it a worthy trade-off. And what about hunters, fishermen, and nature enthusiasts whose pre-dawn thrills are part of their sport? An expected reward drives them.

Others deny themselves every nonessential purchase in order to save for an anniversary cruise or a house or graduate school. And what about the grapefruit and cottage cheese diet? (I don't recommend it.) The prize in the distance spurs on the hopeful.

The flip side involves discipline to avoid a negative consequence. Waking up every two hours to give medicine to a sick toddler, grueling physical therapy after a knee replacement, studying for exams—all require discipline.

Compare memorizing Scripture to a daily regimen of walking—it's not difficult, complicated, or expensive, and there's no athletic ability required. When we hear of someone who walks three miles a day, this impresses us, but not because of the person's skill. We could all do this if we chose to. And that's the point. We admire them because they choose to exercise. We esteem those individuals who choose to discipline themselves for a desired result, in this case, good health.

The apostle Paul exhorts his protégé Timothy, and all of us, to discipline ourselves for a higher purpose: "Discipline yourself for the purpose of godliness; for bodily discipline is only of little profit, but godliness is profitable for all things, since it holds promise for the present life and also for the life to come" (1 Timothy 4:7–8 NASB).

Go after that prize, and you will not be disappointed in this life or in the next.

Sometimes people we perceive as having great discipline falter in other areas unknown to us. A short conversation with my husband would enlighten you to the fact that my housekeeping chores lack discipline. My oven hasn't been cleaned since I moved into this townhouse six years ago. I don't care. I don't want to clean the oven. I'm undisciplined. And worse yet, it's a self-cleaning oven. I'm just too lazy to turn it on. It's pathetic! No more examples.

Do not look at me or someone else and wish you had that other person's discipline. Instead pray for an appetite so intense that nothing else will satisfy.

I suggest trying some short-term discipline as a test to see if the payoff proves worthy. That's what this chapter holds for you—a thirty-day experiment in disciplining yourself, enticed by the promise of a greater reward.

We will now take on chapters 2 and 3 of Titus. I'll walk you through the first ten days.

Day 1
— ◆ —

TITUS 2 : 1

You must teach what is in accord with sound doctrine.

- ◆ Begin with verse 1. It's so short, you should have it down before you get out of the shower.

- ◆ Think about what the verse says, who says it, and to whom.

- ◆ Ask yourself, What is sound doctrine? What is not sound doctrine?

- ◆ Review and meditate on each word. Is this verse also applicable to women's Bible studies? Mothers teaching their children? Men teaching other men?

- ◆ Make this verse a prayer to God that you will speak and teach what is in accord with sound doctrine.

- ◆ Reflect on the word *must*. What if Titus does not teach what is in accord with sound doctrine? What if you do not?

- ◆ Ask God to teach you sound doctrine through your time in the book of Titus.

- ◆ Carry these words with you throughout the day.

◆ Review periodically while driving or waiting, at lunch, or on a break at work.

◆ Come back to these words before bedtime. Secure them in your mind.

Day 2

— ◆ —

TITUS 2:2

Teach the older men to be temperate, worthy of respect, self-controlled, and sound in faith, in love and in endurance.

◆ When your alarm goes off, give your first thoughts to yesterday's verse. Have you got it?

◆ Today's verse is longer, so take it phrase by phrase.

◆ Work on it while you're getting dressed, making coffee, and eating breakfast.

◆ Ask yourself questions. Who is Titus supposed to be teaching? What is he to teach them?

◆ Why do older men need these qualities? Think about their roles in society and in a church.

◆ Keep saying this verse over and over.

◆ Define the words that describe what the older man should be.

◆ Take your verses with you as you go about your day.

◆ Say verses 1 and 2 together. It may take fifteen or twenty times to remember these verses.

◆ Don't forget to review before you go to bed.

Day 3

TITUS 2:3

*Likewise, teach the older women to be reverent
in the way they live, not to be slanderers or addicted
to much wine, but to teach what is good.*

◆ When you awaken, review your first two verses.

◆ Move on to today's verse. Take it phrase by phrase, or line by line.

◆ Who is this verse about? How should they behave and why?

◆ Make this verse a plea to God for yourself and for others you know.

◆ Think and meditate on God's reasons behind this instruction to Titus.

◆ Review all three of your verses while you're busy about your day.

◆ After work, keep your verses on the kitchen counter while you cook dinner and clean up.

◆ Review during the evening hours and before you go to bed.

Day 4

TITUS 2:4

*Then they can train the younger women
to love their husbands and children,*

◆ Get out of bed thinking about God and His invaluable Word. Review your three verses.

◆ Tackle today's verse, another short one. What is God saying here?

◆ Notice the connection to yesterday's verse. Today we get the reason behind verse 3.

◆ We hear a lot of talk these days about mentoring. This is where it comes from—Titus.

◆ Say all four verses over and over as you reflect on their meaning.

◆ Pray this verse for the young women that you know.

◆ These four verses will take less than thirty seconds to review. Time can be found.

◆ Use waiting time to review: at the bank, at the fast-food drive-thru, at the dentist.

◆ Come back to these words before bed. Then drift off to sleep, thinking and praying.

Day 5
— ◆ —

TITUS 2:5

to be self-controlled and pure, to be busy at home,
to be kind, and to be subject to their husbands,
so that no one will malign the word of God.

◆ Take the first thirty seconds of your day to review your progress. Then go on to verse 5.

◆ Today's verse is so very practical. Proceed slowly and thoroughly. You don't want to miss a word.

◆ Think about the what, why, and how in these instructions.

◆ Concentrate on the words, going over them again and again.

◆ Review as you drive your children to school, or as you drive to work, or wherever you go.

◆ What does this verse say will happen if young women don't do these things? Think about it.

- Share these words with a friend who also needs that encouragement.
- Keep saying this verse out loud, speaking words of exhortation to yourself.
- Make these words a prayer to God for the younger women in your life.
- Come back often to today's verse, working to implant it into your memory for future use.
- Remember to review before you go to bed. This will guard your thought life.

Day 6

TITUS 2:6

Similarly, encourage the young men to be self-controlled.

- It's a new day with a new verse. Start with the previous five and then move on to verse 6.
- Recite today's verse at least ten times while getting ready for the day.
- Keep the TV off and review verses instead.
- Are you seeing any similarities in Paul's instructions to different people? What and why?
- Review all six verses while you walk the dog, or walk yourself, or push the baby stroller.
- Think about what the church would be like if we all obeyed these instructions.
- Keep your mind and heart surrendered to God's thoughts. Is He teaching you something?
- Come back at lunch to feast on God's Word. Take every thought captive.

- Mundane chores and errands become joyful when you include Scripture review.
- Conclude your day by rehearsing what God is teaching you in His Word.

Day 7

—— ◆ ——

TITUS 2:7

In everything set them an example by doing what is good.
In your teaching show integrity, seriousness

- Discipline yourself to give your first thoughts to God.
- Review what you've learned so far. See if you can do it all without looking. Then jump into verse 7.
- Today's verse includes when and who and how and what. Look for these.
- Keep reviewing throughout the day. Learn to recite Scripture while doing other things.
- You're up to about forty-five seconds. Try to fit in several review times.
- Say the words out loud so you can hear them. This aids the learning process.
- End your day with God's Word. Don't forget: The blessing comes from meditating day and night.

Day 8

—— ◆ ——

TITUS 2:8

and soundness of speech that cannot be condemned,
so that those who oppose you may be ashamed
because they have nothing bad to say about us.

◆ Wake up to a new day eager for more of God's truth. Go over your seven verses.

◆ Can you see God's character in the things He commands for us?

◆ Today's verse gives a why for the previous verse. Our reputation depends on our obedience.

◆ But how can we obey what we don't know? That's why we're learning God's instructions.

◆ Let this verse become a prayer to God to build in you an impeccable character and a sterling reputation so God will be exalted by your life. He wants to honor that kind of prayer.

◆ Say your verses over and over.

◆ Find a kindred spirit to share what God is teaching you.

◆ Give God your full attention at day's end. Thank Him that His Word will not return void.

Day 9

—— ◆ ——

TITUS 2:9

Teach slaves to be subject to their masters in everything, to try to please them, not to talk back to them,

◆ It's another day to learn something new. Start by reviewing your eight previous verses.

◆ Add today's verse, line by line. You are establishing such good habits. Congratulate yourself.

◆ Though we do not live in a society with slaves, how else might this verse apply?

◆ Ask God for insights as you go over and over these words.

◆ Come back throughout your day. Take one-minute breaks for God's Word.

◆ Tell someone what you are learning: your spouse, your kids, your friend. They need it too.

◆ Have your verses with you wherever you go. You never know when you'll have a spare moment.

◆ Household chores are more enjoyable when combined with Scripture. And the time goes by more quickly.

◆ Always come back to God's Word before bed. If you're too exhausted, just read the words.

Day 10

TITUS 2:10

and not to steal from them, but to show that they can be fully trusted, so that in every way they will make the teaching about God our Savior attractive.

◆ Begin your day with God. Don't miss a single day. Review while doing other things.

◆ Add your new verse. You are up to one-minute review time for chapter 2.

◆ Look at your verses over breakfast.

◆ Ask questions pertaining to this verse. The life of an obedient and trusted slave would attract others to the Savior. Can this apply to us as well?

◆ Pray about your lifestyle. Ask God to make you an attractive witness for Him.

◆ Find one-minute slots in your day to go over these ten verses.

◆ Recite your verses in the car, in a traffic jam. Turn off the radio and listen to God instead.

◆ Repeat the ten verses when you crawl into bed after a full day.

Day 11

— ◆ —

TITUS 2:1 1

*For the grace of God that brings
salvation has appeared to all men.*

Day 12

— ◆ —

TITUS 2:1 2

*It teaches us to say "No" to ungodliness and
worldly passions, and to live self-controlled,
upright and godly lives in this present age,*

Day 13

— ◆ —

TITUS 2:1 3

*while we wait for the blessed hope—the glorious appearing
of our great God and Savior, Jesus Christ,*

Day 14

— ◆ —

TITUS 2:1 4

*who gave himself for us to redeem us from all wickedness
and to purify for himself a people that are his very own, eager
to do what is good.*

Day 15

— ◆ —

TITUS 2:15

These, then, are the things you should teach.
Encourage and rebuke with all authority.
Do not let anyone despise you.

Day 16

— ◆ —

TITUS 3:1

Remind the people to be subject to rulers and authorities,
to be obedient, to be ready to do whatever is good,

Day 17

— ◆ —

TITUS 3:2

to slander no one, to be peaceable and considerate,
and to show true humility toward all men.

Day 18

— ◆ —

TITUS 3:3

At one time we too were foolish, disobedient,
deceived and enslaved by all kinds of passions
and pleasures. We lived in malice and envy,
being hated and hating one another.

Day 19

— ◆ —

TITUS 3:4

But when the kindness and
love of God our Savior appeared,

Day 20

— ◆ —

TITUS 3:5

he saved us, not because of righteous things we had done,
but because of his mercy. He saved us through the washing
of rebirth and renewal by the Holy Spirit,

Day 21

— ◆ —

TITUS 3:6

whom he poured out on us generously
through Jesus Christ our Savior,

Day 22

— ◆ —

TITUS 3:7

so that, having been justified by his grace, we
might become heirs having the hope of eternal life.

Day 23

TITUS 3:8

This is a trustworthy saying. And I want you to stress these
things, so that those who have trusted in God may be
careful to devote themselves to doing what is good.
These things are excellent and profitable for everyone.

Day 24

TITUS 3:9

But avoid foolish controversies and genealogies
and arguments and quarrels about the law,
because these are unprofitable and useless.

Day 25

TITUS 3:10

Warn a divisive person once, and then warn him
a second time. After that, have nothing to do with him.

Day 26

TITUS 3:11

You may be sure that such a man is warped
and sinful; he is self-condemned.

Day 27

TITUS 3:12

As soon as I send Artemas or Tychicus to you,
do your best to come to me at Nicopolis,
because I have decided to winter there.

Day 28

TITUS 3:13

Do everything you can to help Zenas the lawyer and Apollos
on their way and see that they have everything they need.

Day 29

TITUS 3:14

Our people must learn to devote themselves to doing
what is good, in order that they may provide for daily
necessities and not live unproductive lives.

Day 30

TITUS 3:15

Everyone with me sends you greetings. Greet those
who love us in the faith. Grace be with you all.

Hurray! You've crossed the finish line. Well done! Enjoy the satisfaction that discipline brings. You plodded along, slow and steady, and nourished your soul each step of the way. You chose God as your companion, to be with you and in you.

Now that you know the words in your head, keep praying that God will take these truths and transcribe them onto your heart. Live like a recipient of God's kindness and mercy. Live like one who waits for the blessed hope, the appearing of your great God and Savior, who gave Himself for you.

So where do you go from here? First, take the next few days, even up to a week, to review the entire book of Titus each day. Recite Titus, in its entirety, in the morning or at night, or whenever you can fit it in during your day. It only takes six to seven minutes to review. Break it down into chapters if you need to, but there is a benefit to saying it all together. Ask your spouse or a friend to listen while you go through it. This will help the text to gel in your mind and give you confidence that you know it. And it will encourage the listener more than you can imagine.

DESIRE AND DISCIPLINE

A fourth-grade class at a Christian school in Orlando took on a memorization project, the book of James. It worked like this. The 108 verses in James were divided into the thirty-six weeks in a school year, which breaks down to three verses per week. The class spent a few minutes each day learning their new verse and reviewing old ones.

By the end of the school year, every one of these children could recite the entire book of James, and they did so in an evening church service in front of their proud parents and congregation. What a witness! These nine- and ten-year-olds accomplished much more than memory work. They implanted God's Word into their hearts and lives. They could have memorized 108 separate, unrelated verses, but a wise teacher saw the value of learning an entire book. I was so impressed to hear about this, I knew you would be too.

I return to the subject of desire and discipline. We all experience times when desire wanes and discipline caves. Waiting for the gumption to get going only confirms our indifference and brings on self-flagellation. When this occurs, and it will, it shows us an ugly reality—that within ourselves we can't even muster up a love for God. It has to come from Him. Only God can free us from self-absorption and turn us in a God-ward direction.

I share with you a prayer from A. W. Tozer's classic book *The Pursuit of God*. I have these words taped inside my personal prayer book to keep me praying with a humble and hungry heart. I invite you to do the same.

> O God, I have tasted Thy goodness, and it has both satisfied me and made me thirsty for more. I am painfully conscious of my need of further grace. I am ashamed of my lack of desire. O God, the Triune God, I want to want Thee; I long to be filled with longing; I thirst to be made more thirsty still. Show me Thy glory, I pray Thee, that so I may know Thee indeed. Begin in mercy a new work of love within me. Say to my soul, "Rise up, my love, my fair one, and come away." Then give me grace to rise and follow Thee up from this misty lowland where I have wandered so long.
> In Jesus' name, Amen.[2]

8»
THE BENEFITS OF TRANSFORMED THINKING

MY MISSIONARY FRIENDS RICK and Lisa Kellum moved to France nineteen years ago. As they prepared for the mission field, they knew that a prerequisite for successful ministry was mastering the language.

Rick had previously lived in France and had competence in the language. Lisa had neither. When they arrived in France, baby in tow, Lisa enrolled in language school part-time. She became skilled in the basics after months of memorizing vocabulary, verb paradigms, and grammar rules.

She soon realized, however, that communicating with locals required more than this foundation. She had to go beyond verbalizing French words and sentences to actually *thinking* in French.

Every day Rick conversed with students on university campuses, interacted with French people, sharpened his skills, and immersed himself in the culture. Lisa, meanwhile, was isolated at home with a baby, then another, then another. When she went out for ministry events, she nervously attempted to use her language skills, but she was clearly in over her head. She stayed close to Rick, who became her crutch.

After four years of struggling they both knew drastic measures were called for. They moved their family of five to a city where there was a language school. Rick watched the three boys, ages five, three, and six months, while Lisa went to school full-time. Her new environment provided total immersion: reading, writing, and speaking in French only—no English allowed, even on breaks.

She learned to process in French, to recognize and then reproduce the concepts. After a while it became natural. She learned to *think* in French.

Language school, although inconvenient, costly, and time-consuming, proved necessary for Lisa to become fully usable in that culture. After language school the Kellums moved again to a new city and started over, this time equipped.

Scripture memory and even Bible study parallel the Kellums' experience. God wants us to go beyond the building blocks of Bible verses and stories and begin to *think biblically* because we can't *live biblically* unless we do. Memorizing verses doesn't automatically translate into successful Christian living. You have to learn to *think biblically*, and the only way to do that is total *immersion* in the Scriptures.

I've become passionate about this issue. I will give you a brief summary of the reasons *why* we need transformed thinking, *what* transformed thinking looks like, and *how* we get there.

WHY WE NEED TRANSFORMED THINKING

Thinking matters. Every day we live out what we believe, and our belief depends on what we think. I see four areas that negatively influence how we think: culture, pseudo-Christian realities, Satan, and ourselves.

Culture

Our twenty-first-century society values—among other things—individual choice, personalized spirituality, and tolerance for all beliefs. Suspicion of traditional institutions makes us skeptical of conventional wisdom. We obsess with celebrities and allow them undue influence.

Welcome and unwelcome messages permeate every aspect of our lives, and no innate skills exist to discern what's helpful and what's harmful: TV, Internet, iTunes, Facebook, movies, Twitter, book clubs, SiriusXM radio. Our surroundings dictate what to value, how to live, what to think, and what to reject as unthinkable. Clever arguments persuade the unsuspecting, and philosophies of the cosmos guide the learned. The world misleads with Photoshopped realities. Make no mistake: This culture intends to squeeze us into its mold and will bully us until we fit in.

The apostle Paul warned the Colossians, "See to it that no one takes you captive through hollow and deceptive philosophy, which depends on human tradition and the basic principles of this world rather than on Christ" (Colossians 2:8). Christians have been given a blueprint, a standard to live by, that collides with the philosophies of our culture. En masse, Christians are backing away from their biblical convictions and surrendering to the latest ideologies. And many Christians who want to stay true to their faith don't know how to integrate the Bible with everyday life. Trained to arm themselves by quoting Scripture, suddenly those verses seem irrelevant for our new world.

Pseudo-Christian Realities

Christians employ many avenues to get their message out: Sunday services, TV programming, Internet, Ebooks, etc. The unsuspecting Christian assumes an uncorrupted, untainted message, but buyer, beware! Not everything in the sacred realm is sanctified.

Not everyone who claims Christ as his or her God of choice is indeed Christian. False teachers abound, some with best-selling books, a large viewing audience, and/or convention-sized auditoriums.

Most false teachers use Bible verses. They love to cut-and-paste the Bible to create the god they worship and the doctrines they espouse. Lies, disguised in half-truths, lure in the naïve and trusting. Many fall prey to the insidious teachings of health, wealth, and power. So-called Christian groups have equal access to all media, so only the discerning manage to separate fact from fiction.

Paul described false teachers as "enemies of the cross of Christ" (Philippians 3:18) and warned the Colossians not to be deceived by "fine-sounding arguments" (Colossians 2:4).

But how will we recognize a watered-down gospel, less-than-sound doctrine, and teaching that is Bible-filled but not biblical? False teachers don't come with a warning sign on their foreheads, and not every John 3:16 placard preaches the same gospel. You may have memorized fifty stand-alone Bible verses, but depending on those alone may not save you from the snare of false doctrine.

Satan

Even with an image considered unsophisticated and ar-chaic, Satan remains an ever-present threat to our well-being.

Satan lured Eve, his first victim, by causing her to doubt God's Word and enticing her to take something forbidden. Adam might have told the serpent to get lost, but his demise came at the suggestion of his wife. They both fell by different means.

Satan had the audacity to quote Scripture to Jesus. He

was unsuccessful, but he targeted the Son of God with what he knew Jesus valued.

Satan doesn't need to change his tactics because they still work. If he can't entice us through our own desires (HGTV, Internet porn, Pinterest) he'll use peer pressure (Facebook, Twitter, celebrity causes), or he'll quote Scripture to us.

The apostle Paul warns us that Satan masquerades as an angel of light, and his servants as servants of *righteousness*. The majority of Christians, clueless to the presence of these impostors, have no discerning ability to identify them or correct them.

Ourselves

Facing endless choices and information overload, we sort through our options. We grab our Bible to look for answers to complex issues, but when we don't find what we're looking for, we conclude that the Bible has nothing to say and in frustration look elsewhere. "I'll just Google it and take my chances."

Lack of training in our churches has left the body of Christ unable to integrate Bible knowledge with everyday life. And sometimes, stand-alone memory verses contribute to this disconnect. (A good example is the verse "I can do everything through Christ who strengthens me." There's a huge disappointment in store for the one who *claims* this verse as it stands on its own.)

Biblical illiteracy takes much of the blame, and rightly so. But compounding that, we don't know how to take modern-day situations, ones not addressed in the Bible, and think them through from a biblical perspective. Some of the contemporary issues that trouble Christians include environmentalism, online-dating, prom-night guidelines, nursing homes, and sticky office predicaments.

Our default mode, "Just trust your heart," sends many down a slippery slope. Proverbs tells us, "He who trusts in his own heart is a fool" (Proverbs 28:26 NASB). Ignorance and indecision keep many Christians hostage to their own ambivalence.

Each of the four factors intimidates us. Together they overwhelm us.

WHAT TRANSFORMED THINKING LOOKS LIKE

The descriptions of these four pitfalls of negative influence reveal *why* we need transformed thinking. So what is transformed thinking, and what does it look like? To answer that, let me show you one place where we find transformed thinking in Scripture. My best attempt to condense and paraphrase Romans 12:1–2 follows:

Therefore you Christians, in light of everything God has done for you, the only reasonable response is total dedication to God. Do not allow yourself to be conformed any longer to the values of the present world, but now allow yourself to be continually transformed by the renewing of your mind, so that you will be able to discern the will of God, in order to live out the will of God. (Romans 12:1–2, paraphrased)

Notice the key elements germane to our topic:

- Do not allow yourself to be conformed to the values of the present world.
- Allow yourself to be continually *transformed*. How? By the *renewing of your mind*.
- *So that* you will be able to discern the will of God.
- *In order to* live out the will of God.

Be conformed and *be transformed* are passive verbs in the Greek text.[3] It's something that happens to you. You get conformed to the world. You get transformed by God.

Transformed thinking enables you to *know* the will of God, so that you can *do* the will of God.

Transformed thinking could be described as any of these:

- realigning your thinking to coincide with God's thinking so that your actions reflect God's viewpoint
- reasoning based on God's values so as to recognize the best option to carry out
- integrating biblical principles with everyday situations to come up with the right thing to do

Transformed thinking involves thinking in order to act.

Sometimes the process is intuitive—you know *you shouldn't steal from the company* because that violates God's principles. Sometimes it takes prolonged contemplation to examine all factors, weigh the options, and decipher the priority issues.

HOW DO WE GET TRANSFORMED THINKING?

Transformed thinking comes from *renewing your mind* with Scripture. Continually letting God's Word replace worldly perceptions with His unchanging truth will transform your mind to be more like His.

The reason our minds need transforming comes from Romans 1:28. Speaking of humankind, Paul writes, "Since they did not think it worthwhile to retain the knowledge of God, he gave them over to a depraved mind, to do what ought not to be done."

Notice once again: The mind determines the behavior.

As God renews our minds with Scripture, we begin to think biblically so that we can live biblically. Thinking biblically presupposes Bible knowledge. Without it you have no filter, and nothing to weigh your options against. You cannot come up with God's perspective without understanding God's thoughts expressed in His Word.

Once a trendy question, *What would Jesus do?* is actually a valid way to process a situation you encounter. If you can support your answer with a *why* from Scripture, you are in the ballpark of a good answer. Look for a story, an example, model, or principle in line with God's character and His plan. Be aware that many Bible stories are descriptive, but not prescriptive— Gideon's fleece tells us what *he* did, not what we should do.

Renewing your mind may appear to be a New Testament idea, but it goes way back to the Old Testament. God's explicit requirement for kings sheds light on His mandate and His method for transformed thinking.

> When he takes the throne of his kingdom, he is to write for himself on a scroll a copy of this law, taken from that of the priests, who are Levites. It is to be with him, and he is to read it all the days of his life so that he may learn to revere the Lord his God and follow carefully all the words of this law and these decrees and not consider himself better than his brothers and turn from the law to the right or to the left. Then he and his descendants will reign a long time over his kingdom in Israel. (Deuteronomy 17:18–20)

This continuing education for the king required him to write out his own copy of the book of Deuteronomy. That would take a while (it's thirty-two pages in my Bible). The king must keep the scroll with him. Then he must read it *every day of his life*. That would take something more than an hour a day, even for a speed-reader. God explains His reasons for requiring this: so that the king would learn to revere God (the beginning of wisdom), so that the king would obey all the laws, so that the king would see himself correctly, not elevating himself above the others in his kingdom. If each king of Israel would follow these guidelines, God would prolong their dynasty.

Reading Deuteronomy every day would familiarize the king with the history of Israel, God's character, the Ten Commandments, and other decrees, promises, and warnings. Because the king was God's representative, God wanted the king to think His thoughts and govern as He would. Daily time reviewing the same material over and over would cement God's plan for the nation into the king's mind and become the foundation on which he would live and govern. Sounds like a great plan!

Unfortunately, it is doubtful that any of the kings ever followed this requirement. Their excuses may have sounded like some of ours: "Why should I write out my own copy? There are plenty of other copies around here. Why should I read it today? I read it yesterday, and I already know what it says, and nothing's changed. Got a lot to do today—I'll get to it later."

Consequently, the kings veered to the right and the left, and ultimately God removed them from their position of authority. They didn't *live* as God had prescribed because they didn't *think* as He had prescribed.

Transformed thinking, incremental growth over time,

requires not just exposure to God's Word but *immersion* in it. This time-consuming, long-term commitment flies in the face of our instant-answers culture. I can hear the pushback now: "That will take forever." Yes, it will take a *lifetime*.

In His Word, God reveals His mind, His heart, His plans for His kingdom, and how His people fit into that plan. He tells us, or shows us, how to live as aliens and strangers in this world, while citizens of a heavenly kingdom. As He transforms our thinking, our lives will reflect that.

I don't want to give a false impression that I am now a biblical thinker, able to decipher God's perspective, and know what to do in every situation—that's far from the truth. But after memorizing books and passages for more than twenty years now, I've seen tremendous progress in discernment, and this motivates me to keep at it for more. It comes from abiding in God's Word.

Some situations are intuitive, some take thorough contemplation, and some are a complete mind-boggling mystery, but I'm growing.

Because of the Holy Spirit and God's Word in my life, I'm not chained to my basic temperament—gullible, unsuspicious, and every salesman's best prospect. Apart from the influence of God's Word, I would buy into every prevailing philosophy and float like a leaf down the river.

My highest priority remains a close walk with God. But walking with God means going in the same direction as God, loving the things He loves, and consequently doing the things He does. I can't do that apart from transformed thinking; I wouldn't know what that looks like in my life. Washing my mind over and over with God's Word replaces my perspective with His.

A renewed mind helps evaluate media messages for truth and error.

Transformed thinking allows me to recognize the syncretizing of other religions with Christianity. I notice verses mingled with foreign concepts, and conclusions based on out-of-context assertions. Often I have to chew on it for a while and sort it out piece by piece, but I have the means to achieve that.

Staying in God's Word keeps me alert to Satan's attempts to distort it and to my own weakness in trying to justify myself by it.

I don't want to imply that you have to memorize books of Scripture in order to transform your thinking. I believe that concentrated Bible study (book-by-book, not topic-by-topic) over a prolonged period of time will also transform your thinking. In my life, both studying and memorizing work in tandem. I will say, however, that memorizing books and passages in context *will* transform your thinking.

The apostle Paul's prayers for the churches reveal his grasp of the progression from knowledge to discernment to living accordingly.

> And this is my prayer: that your love may abound more and more in knowledge and depth of insight, *so that you may be able to discern what is best* and may be pure and blameless until the day of Christ. (Philippians 1:9–10, emphasis added)
>
> We have not stopped praying for you and asking God to fill you with the knowledge of his will through all spiritual wisdom and understanding. And we pray this *in order that you may live a life worthy of the Lord and may please him in every way*: bearing fruit in

every good work, growing in the knowledge of God.
(Colossians 1:9–10, emphasis added)

In these two passages Paul mentions *depth of insight* and
spiritual wisdom as the means through which a person determines the right course of action. Paul, also the author of the
Romans passage, makes *depth of insight* and *spiritual wisdom*
synonymous with a renewed mind.

Wisdom is *skill in living*—knowing how to take the
knowledge you have and apply it to your real-life situation.
Teenagers breaking curfew may not be addressed specifically in
the Bible, but wisdom takes truths from Scripture and formu-
lates a plan of action based on those truths.

I have memorized Proverbs 2, 4, and 8. All of them deal
with wisdom: its value, its benefits, and how to attain it. I
cannot choose a favorite but Proverbs 2 illustrates our theme
of transformed thinking. I will give you the first ten verses in
three sections.

> My son, if you accept my words
>   and store up my commands within you,
> turning your ear to wisdom
>   and applying your heart to understanding,
> and if you call out for insight
>   and cry aloud for understanding,
> and if you look for it as for silver
>   and search for it as for hidden treasure,
> then you will understand the fear of the Lord
>   and find the knowledge of God. (Proverbs 2:1–5)

Look at the verbs and phrases related to attaining wisdom: *accept my words, store up my commands, turning your ear, applying your heart, call out for, cry aloud for, look for, search for.* The word choices demonstrate active pursuit!

The result? Then you will understand the fear of the Lord (the beginning of wisdom). And you will find the knowledge of God.

> For the Lord gives wisdom,
>   and from his mouth come knowledge and
>   understanding.
> He holds victory in store for the upright,
>   he is a shield to those whose walk is blameless,
> for he guards the course of the just
>   and protects the way of his faithful ones.
> (Proverbs 2:6–8)

This section highlights the Lord as the source of wisdom, knowledge, and understanding.

> Then you will understand what is right and just
>   and fair—every good path.
> For wisdom will enter your heart,
>   and knowledge will be pleasant to your soul.
> (Proverbs 2:9–10)

When we search for wisdom we will understand the right path to take. Wisdom, synonymous with a renewed mind, helps synthesize doctrine and praxis, truth and implementation.

The age we live in presents obstacles on every front. We begin to sort out the confusion, and within a millisecond new challenges hit us. How did God intend for His people to survive a hostile society and represent Him correctly? With renewed minds that know how to live.

God has commissioned His followers as foreign missionaries living on the earth. This requires training in *His* language. With prolonged time and effort in God's Word, its transforming power will renew our minds and enable us to do the will of our Father, so that we can represent Him. God receives the glory when the inhabitants of this planet recognize God's children as citizens of another place.

9»
REVIEW & CHEW

THE QUESTIONS THAT PEOPLE bring to me most often are about review. Though you can address questions and submit tips at our online community (www.janetpope.org/blog/), this chapter will help you understand *why* we should review and provide ideas on *how to review.* I'm also including tips, ideas from other memorizers, reasons for failure, and encouragement for the long haul.

WHY REVIEW?

Meditation

Simply stated: reviewing keeps me chewing. Memorizing and reviewing Scripture makes meditation possible. And that's how we become like the man in Psalm 1, continually nourished, yielding fruit in season, and successfully equipped for God's agenda. When we don't meditate on God's Word, we often walk away unmoved and unchanged.

In Paul's second letter to Timothy (2 Timothy 2:3–7), he gives three images: an active-duty soldier, a competing athlete, and a hardworking farmer. Then Paul tells Timothy, "Reflect on what I am saying, for the Lord will give you insight into all this." God wants us to take the teachings in His Word and ponder them deeply. *What exactly did God mean? Why did He use that example? How does that relate to me?* The Holy Spirit gives insight into the text as we think through the words, the illustrations, the implications. Meditation on God's Word brings insight from God Himself.

Long-term Memory

One of my goals in reviewing is to move the Scriptures from short-term memory to long-term memory. Let's look at the difference. When memorizing Scripture, anyone can remember a verse, short-term. If you repeat a verse fifteen to twenty times in one day, you'll be able to recall it the next day. Moving Scripture from short-term memory to long-term memory works the same way you move other information—by repetition. No magical or mysterious method exists.

When speaking on this subject, I like to ask the audience for a show of hands: "How many of you know the *pledge of allegiance to the flag,* by memory?" Virtually everyone over thirty who grew up in the United States raises a hand. "So how did you accomplish that? You recited it in school five days a week for twelve years. Will you ever forget it? Probably not, because it's now stored in long-term memory. It's ready to recite whenever the occasion presents itself."

The same principle applies to Scripture memory. Repetition over a prolonged period of time will move information from short-term to long-term memory and will make those truths available to you whenever you need them. When the moment arises, it's already there, stored for your retrieval.

Negative Thinking

Reviewing Scripture helps to override all the negative things we store in our heads. Our minds often prove to be our own worst enemies because bad memories take up a lot of storage space. Our minds get weighed down by negativity, relationships-gone-bad, regrets, poor choices, years wasted, ir-retrievable words, hurts that won't heal—it's a never-ending list. These negative thoughts play over and over and over, like

CDs on auto-repeat in our minds. They fence us in and chain us to our past. We lie down to sleep, and they replay in our heads. We walk around in a daze while morose thoughts take hold. We turn on some noise to drown out our own hurts and fears. Making an impact on the world gets pushed off the feasibility list; we just want escape from our own bad dreams.

I have my own set of negative CDs I replay in my mind: the if-onlys, the what-ifs, the I-wish-I-hadn'ts. Since the past cannot be changed, I can feel locked in and spiral downward. Scripture meditation to the rescue! I cannot change the past, but I can change the channel. I don't have to dwell on mistakes and regrets. My other option fills my mind with God's grace for the past, His power for the present, and His presence always.

I run to the Psalms, to words stored in my mind. I say them aloud and rejuvenate my soul.

> Shout with joy to God all the earth!
>> Sing the glory of his name;
>> make his praise glorious!
> Say to God, "How awesome are your deeds!
>> So great is your power
>> that your enemies cringe before you.
> All the earth bows down to you;
>> they sing praise to you;
>> they sing praise to your name."
> Come and see what God has done,
>> how awesome his works in man's behalf!"
> (Psalm 66:1–5)

These words breathe life into my spirit, and I rise up to praise Him. He increases, while I decrease. My mind's pessimism bows in allegiance to the One who redeems me from the pit. Courage wells up, and I refuse to cower in defeat. Truth strengthens me, and joy revives me. I run to God's Word and embrace victory in the moment. Many turn to alcohol or drugs or mind-numbing computer games as an antidote for sadness; I turn to God's Word, and it never disappoints.

Reviewing and chewing have saved many desperate days.

HOW TO REVIEW

Long-term you will need to find a review system that fits you. Every few years I tweak my system to make it work better for me. These suggestions will get you started. I will begin with my *old* system, then explain my *new* system, then give you some twenty-first-century adaptations.

Old System: Great for the First Seven Passages

After memorizing any book or passage (such as Titus), choose a specific day of the week, and designate that as your weekly review day. For example, on Mondays you will always review Titus. No matter what other passage you are memorizing that day, you will review Titus every Monday. That means that at the end of a year you will have reviewed Titus fifty-two times, moving it closer to long-term memory.

Your next project might be the book of Philippians. After completing Philippians, designate another day of the week to review Philippians—let's say Tuesdays. Your next completed project will go on Wednesdays. Here is an example:

Monday: Titus
Tuesday: Philippians
Wednesday: Psalm 139
Thursday: 1 Thessalonians
Friday: Psalm 1
Saturday: 1 Corinthians 13

This system works well for seven or fewer passages. Weekly markers keep you reviewing the truth you've learned. After seven passages or books, the system becomes burdensome because you have to double-up on days. Somehow the joy gets lost when it becomes a chore that hangs over you every single day.

New System: Excellent for More than Seven Passages

Once you have more than seven passages to review, this system provides regular accountability without the daily deadlines. Take all the passages/books you have memorized and put them in the natural order that they appear in the Bible. For example:

Ruth
Psalm 139
1 Corinthians 13
Philippians
1 Thessalonians
2 Timothy
Titus
James
1 Peter
2 Peter

Start your review cycle with Ruth. Take *as many days as you need* to review Ruth so that it is firm in your mind. After that, go on to Psalm 139 and take as many days as you need to keep it solid. Follow your list in order. If you skip a day, so be it; it doesn't affect your system. When you get to the end of the list, go back to the beginning and go through the cycle again. When you have a new passage to add, just insert it wherever it fits in Bible order. Doing it this way, you don't have to remember what comes next on your review schedule. Your next review assignment is always whatever comes next in Bible order.

Some passages you will fly through because you know them so well. Others will take a few days. On long books, like Hebrews, I divide the review into manageable segments, chapters 1–4, 5–8, 9–10, 11–13. Some days I review a lot, other days not so much. Completing your review cycle will depend on how many passages you have and how much time you take on each. It's all up to you.

Review System #3

Eventually you will need to tweak the new system again. For me, with forty-seven passages to review, my cycle takes more than nine months to go through, and by that time I've lost some of my *recently* memorized passages. An easy solution works for me. Alternate your newest passage with all of your other passages. For example, this summer I memorized 2 Thessalonians, so it needs more review or else I will lose it.

Ruth
2 Thessalonians
Psalm 139
2 Thessalonians

1 Corinthians 13
2 Thessalonians
Philippians
2 Thessalonians

When I feel as if 2 Thessalonians is solidifying in my memory, maybe after six months or a year, I insert it in the proper place (Bible order) and review it like the rest of my passages. By that time I may have another new passage to alternate.

Twenty-First-Century Adaptations

Although I still use the 3 x 5 index card spirals, others successfully use iPads, iPhones, Kindles, and the like. The review systems work the same way, but the Scripture is either on your phone or somewhere else. When I choose to use my iPad, I go to the Bible app, and automatically 2 Thessalonians comes up because I have programmed it to do so.

The same can be done on your phone or any notebook or tablet. Most people take their phone everywhere they go, so if you have a smartphone, you will always have your Bible with you. You won't forget to take your phone, but you might forget to take your spiral with the index cards.

There are a few disadvantages to modern technologies. First, they are dependent on hot spots; you can't download from everywhere. For example, there are airplane limitations. A second would be the occasional dead battery, when you've forgotten to recharge the phone. A third disadvantage is not being able to put markings on your phone app (but you can mark up your Kindle).

Our online community (see www.janetpope.org/blog/)

will also be giving updates on ways to use new technologies for Scripture memory.

Bible websites allow you to select a passage in any version, along with font size, and then print it. There are several advantages to this system. You can mark up the text, drawing circles or underlining trouble spots. You can also write things you are learning in the margins. When your pages get worn out, you can print fresh copies. You can also print multiple copies, one for your house, one for your car, or your office, or wherever you spend a lot of time. Keep them in a pile, or a file, in the order you review.

When walking on a treadmill, printed full pages are much easier than 3 x 5 spirals that require you to flip pages frequently while walking.

Adapt the System to You

My system has evolved as my life has changed. For years I was a stay-home mom with small children, then with teenagers; then I had an empty nest; then I was a full-time student; and now I'm working full-time with a home office. Looking back, I realize I had the most time for memorizing as a stay-home mom with teenagers. I memorized while doing household chores, errands, and a vast amount of waiting at sports practices, piano lessons, carpool lines, doctors, dentists, and orthodontists. I had the least amount of time when I was a full-time seminary student because I needed to spend a lot of memorizing time on Greek and Hebrew vocabulary words, along with a plethora of dates and names I would be tested on. During the five years I was in seminary I did not memorize any new books of the Bible. I adapted my goals. I kept reviewing my other books and only memorized short passages that were manageable for me at that time. Now as a full-time worker, I'm still trying to find my rhythm.

During the first ten years, I memorized approximately ninety chapters. During the second ten years, I memorized fifty chapters. I don't take on new passages as quickly because I have a lot more to review now.

You need to adapt my suggestions to your particular lifestyle. You will be more confident and less frustrated if you devise your own system that works for you. And then you need to keep adapting as your lifestyle changes. When do you have small segments of time? At home, in the car, at the soccer field? Airports and airplanes? Subway? Do you exercise? Walk the dog? Do you spend a lot of time waiting?

Find the pace that works for you. Some people enjoy pushing themselves to do a verse a day. For some, that pace would push them off the cliff. I work well with deadlines, but I also allow myself breaks whenever I need them. Experiment, try different ways, and find your own pace. Then keep adapting as your life changes.

Cathy's Catch-up Review

One of my friends in Pennsylvania found herself frustrated with all the passages she had to review. Without a specific system, she fell behind and began losing some of the books she had worked so hard to learn. She needed to do some catch-up. She wrote to me, delighted that she had devised a system for the next few months to get her back on track.

She took short passages and the Sermon on the Mount and assigned them to August.

Week 1: several psalms

Week 2: Jude

Week 3: 1 Corinthians 13

Week 4: Matthew 5–7

Then she took three books and spread them out over
    four months.

September: 1 Peter, daily review

October: Philippians, daily review

November: Ephesians 1–3, daily review

December: Ephesians 4–6, daily review

This plan, tailor-made for her, allowed her to catch up on
all her review. When she completes the cycle, she can either
repeat it or adapt it to her current needs. I love what else she
wrote: "How special it is to bring back into my heart my past
memory work. While in 1 Peter I felt like I was reopening a
beloved gift." If you find yourself falling behind in reviewing
your passages, put together a plan like Cathy did.

TIPS I'VE LEARNED ALONG THE WAY

Start Out Small

Don't try to tackle the book of Galatians if you've never
memorized passages before. I recommend a very short passage, like Psalm 1. With only six verses, it is doable for everyone and also motivational because it highlights the person
who meditates on God's Word day and night. And it only
takes *one minute* to review. When first beginning to memorize, you haven't yet found large slices of time in your schedule, but you can always find one-minute slices. This trains you
to look for more. If you already know Psalm 1, choose another
short psalm, like Psalm 121.

Which Version

Which version should you memorize? Any version you like. I recommend avoiding a paraphrase. If you choose the version you are the most familiar with, the memorization work will be easier. You can change versions from project to project, but it will be simpler to stay with the same version.

A Verse Per Day of the Month

A helpful way to keep on track is to begin on the first day of a month, memorizing one verse per day. Then follow the days of the month, and you will always know what verse you are on. This works well with most of the New Testament letters or the Psalms because they usually have twenty or twenty-one verses. When you finish on day twenty or twenty-one, spend the rest of the month reviewing before moving on to the next chapter on the first day of the next month. This does not work with the Gospels or the book of Acts because the number of verses per chapter exceeds the number of days in a month.

Balance Multi-chapter Books with Short Projects

After memorizing a several-chapter book or passage, take a month or two to review and chew before moving on. Then choose something *short* for your next project: a psalm, a proverb, a parable, a stand-alone chapter like 1 Corinthians 13. This gives you a breather from the commitment required by a longer book.

Take Enough Time to Review Long Books

Long books like Romans or Hebrews or Esther require either a large block of time for review, or they can be broken down into smaller chunks and reviewed over several days.

Recite

Recite to listeners. Ask friends, a spouse, or your kids if they will read the passage while you recite it, in order to check your progress. There is a double benefit here, for you and the listener. Share your passage with anyone who will listen. Don't keep it to yourself.

Find a Memorizing Partner

Memorizing with someone else adds an accountability dimension that keeps many on track. You and your friend might be memorizing the same passage or different ones. You can recite together on a designated schedule, over the phone, or in person.

Memorize in the Car

Most of us spend a lot of time in our cars, on both short and long trips. Here is the way I redeem that time. On long trips I review long books. Revelation takes more than an hour to review. I can start at the beginning and go all the way through, or I can break it up into sections. For in-town driving, I review short passages. I have two spirals reserved just for short passages (mostly Psalms and Proverbs). I keep these two spirals in my car at all times. When I head out in my car I start where I left off the last time. I have twenty-one passages, each taking 1–3 minutes of review time. You can also review books, one chapter at a time. Memorizing in the car keeps you spiritually refreshed, even when stuck in traffic. This also works on public transportation—maybe even better.

Listen to the Bible

You might listen to Scripture on an audio download or a CD. I tried this many years ago, and it didn't work for me. I think I need to hear myself saying the words out loud and found I had to stop too often to make keeping up with the recording feasible. But it may work for you, so give it a try. Just make sure the audio version matches the version you memorize in!

Combine Memory Work with Bible Study and Personal Devotional Time

Your Scripture memory work does not have to be separate from your daily time with God. Years ago I kept it separate, but no longer. I've learned over time that it's more beneficial to go deeply into one book of the Bible than to read several others. Let your interpretation questions drive you to study the book you are memorizing. Take notes or journal what you're learning. Pray through what you're memorizing for yourself and others.

Build the Bible's Variety into Your Choice of What's Next

Many agonize over what to memorize next, trying to *match* life circumstances with a passage of Scripture, but this isn't always necessary. Remember Job. In his great suffering, God's answer to him didn't address suffering at all. God revealed *Himself* to Job, and that was enough. All scriptural books have value. Choose a variety of topics, authors, and styles to give you a wide spectrum of knowledge. By memorizing from different authors, you will get distinct, though complementary, perspectives and insights. Notice, for example the different authors in these passages and books:

- Matthew 5–7 (Sermon on the Mount): Matthew, quoting Jesus
- Philippians: Paul
- 1 Peter: Peter
- Luke 1–2: Luke
- Hebrews: author unknown
- Isaiah 55: Isaiah
- Psalm 62: David
- Deuteronomy 5–6: Moses

Choose both poetry and prose. Choose some history, prophecy, biography, and doctrine. Choose both Old and New Testaments. Choose something from the Law, the Prophets, and the Psalms. Choose passages you want to meditate on. Each book has a purpose and a unique role in conveying God's character and plan. Notice the great variety in memory projects you might choose:

- *Ruth* is Old Testament history, biography, and prose, from an unknown author.
- *Ecclesiastes* is Old Testament wisdom literature, a mixture of poetry and prose, and Solomon is the generally accepted author.
- *Acts 6:8–7:60*: Stephen's defense contains both New Testament history and Old Testament history. The author of the account is Luke.
- *Hosea* is Old Testament prophecy written as poetry. The author is Hosea.
- *Proverbs 8* is Old Testament wisdom literature. The theme is *wisdom personified.*
- *Mark 14:3–9 and Luke 7:36–50* contain two similar

but distinct stories from the life of Jesus, written by two different authors. Two different women poured perfume on Jesus. Notice their similarities and their differences. Jesus used each one as an example to others.

- *Jesus' four discourses*: Sermon on the Mount (Matthew 5–7), Upper Room (John 13–17), Olivet discourse (Matthew 24), parables of the kingdom (Matthew 13). These are teaching passages, written by two different authors recording Jesus' teaching content.

What **Not** to Memorize

I offer a few cautions to spare you frustration once you've already started a memory project. Some books or passages are so similar to others that memorizing *both* requires intense concentration and easily becomes confusing and defeating.

My advice: Choose one or the other, but not both of these:

- Ephesians or Colossians
- 1 Timothy or Titus
- 2 Peter or Jude
- Sermon on the Mount: Matthew 5–7 or Luke 6

I would also caution beginners from taking on the book of 1 John. It can be tricky with *Dear children* appearing nine times and *Dear friends* six times.

REASONS FOR FAILURE

Many fail because they try to *add* Scripture memory to their already-packed schedule. With no more hours in your day, something has to be eliminated. Your greatest probability of success will be if you learn to incorporate Scripture memory into things you are *already doing*. For example, if you regularly work out at a gym and spend thirty minutes of that time on the treadmill, use that time to memorize (instead of watching TV or listening to music). You can cover a lot of Scripture in thirty minutes. As time goes on, you can drop some things from your schedule to fit in more time for memorizing God's Word.

People have told me their greatest temptation to quit comes when they get tangled in certain words and phrases and can't seem to sort them out. I hear you. What I've learned is that the brain is able to memorize two things at once—a verse and a visual. I've come up with solutions that help me when I hit a kink or a snag in the memorization work: links for kinks, and flags for snags.

Links for Kinks

I've memorized 1 Peter and Ephesians. Both give instructions to slaves, which can be confusing when it comes to review:

Slaves, obey your earthly masters with respect and fear
(Ephesians 6:5)
Slaves, submit yourselves to your masters with all respect
(1 Peter 2:18)

It's easy to get these phrases that begin with *Slaves* mixed up and say the wrong one, and then suddenly you're reciting from a different book—frustrating! The way I overcome this is to look for something to link the verse to so that I can remember which one goes with which.

In 1 Peter, I link *slaves, submit yourselves* (2:18) to an earlier verse that includes *Submit yourselves* (2:13). That repeated phrase becomes my link. I circle each and then draw a line connecting them. I create a visual link on that page. Then when I'm reviewing, I come to *Slaves* and visualize the link.

In Ephesians 6, I link *Slaves, obey* (6:5) to an earlier verse, *Children, obey* (6:1). The word *obey* creates the link. I put circles around the phrases and draw a line connecting them. I create a visual link on that page. When I'm reviewing it, I see the visual link and remember.

Find something you can link, whether it's words, first letters of words, any pattern that you see. On a Bible app, you can highlight if you can't draw lines and circles.

Flags for Snags

When I cannot find any kind of link, my other option is to memorize a caution FLAG that I draw next to the verse, telling me to pause, and think it out. Check out these two easily mixed-up phrases:

Here is a trustworthy saying (2 Timothy 2:11)
This is a trustworthy saying (Titus 3:8)

Every time I say either of these verses, I see a flag in my head, and it causes me to pause and think, "What comes next?"

You can come up with all sorts of ways to remember, but what is encouraging is that the brain can memorize two things at once. The brain can learn words and picture links or flags at the same time.

TIPS FROM OTHER MEMORIZERS

I have asked friends from around the country to give you their thoughts on memorizing and reviewing and when and where they fit it in.

Elizabeth

My friend Elizabeth says, "When memorizing New Testament letters I skip the greetings and the closings because they're all so similar that they frustrate me and bog me down, making me want to quit. And Janet told me I was *free* to do it any way that works for me!"

Tammy

"I memorize straight out of my Bible," reports my friend Tammy. "Then on Saturdays I write out from memory the verses I learned that week, checking my accuracy. Then I journal about what God is teaching me through that passage."

Lise

Lise, an attorney, prints out her verses from her computer. Then she rolls up the pages and takes them with her while jogging. She uses this time to learn new verses and review old ones. She also reviews at the baseball park, where she spends a lot of time with her two teenage sons.

Sue

Sue, a flight attendant, memorizes before she leaves for work and then takes her 3 x 5 spiral to work. She reviews while sitting in her jump seat during takeoffs and landings.

Rob

Rob, an accountant, memorizes and reviews while shaving and getting ready in the morning and while doing yard work like mowing the lawn. He says, "My neighbors think I talk to myself, but whatever!"

Cheryl

Cheryl, a police officer, reviews while on vehicle patrol or foot patrol, while waiting in court or waiting for tow trucks to clear an accident or disabled vehicle. She uses 3 x 5 cards, which she laminates. They fit in her uniform pocket.

Angie

Angie, a physician, sees patients nonstop all day with barely a moment to take a breath. She memorizes in the morning and at night. She says that throughout the day, God brings His Word back to her mind, even without her conscious effort. In the past two years she has memorized Psalm 1, Titus, Psalm 150, and Psalm 103. These verses keep her meditating and close to God.

Shari

Shari, a homeschooling mom, memorizes passages with her teenage boys and her husband, and also works on passages of her own.

Bruce

Bruce, a retired military officer, says, "I memorize while on my four-mile daily walk. It makes the miles go by quickly. But most of all I like the peace and wisdom that come from having His Word in my head and heart."

Marisa

"What better way to think throughout my day, than on God's Word! I recite verses as I apply makeup and get ready for the day. When I wash and dry my thick hair, I realize I have at least twenty uninterrupted (usually boring) minutes to focus on God and His truths," says my friend Marisa, enthusiastically. "Memorizing God's Word has been a huge blessing in my life. I find I focus more on God and His truths and less on my circumstances, which helps me worry less and strengthens my faith. Also, the passages I memorize become very personal to me."

Debbie

Debbie is a rural-route mail carrier, and she works on verses while driving from one stop to the next. She admits that occasionally she has been so focused on her verses that she has missed a few mailboxes and had to make a U-turn! Memorizing brings joy to an otherwise routine job.

ENCOURAGEMENT FOR THE LONG HAUL

"While life often gets in the way, I always miss the discipline of Scripture memory when I don't keep it up," writes Cathy, a busy mom in Louisiana. "I return to it again and again. I'm a recovering perfectionist. It's good to strive for perfection in many things, but in my opinion Scripture memory is not one of them. It's okay if my plan is to memorize a verse a day yet I end up learning only one verse for the week. The result is still the same. The important thing is that I redeem the minutes of my day with meditating on Scripture. The riches that Scripture memory has added to my life are countless (such as an enriched prayer life). That's why when I falter, all that matters is that I return to it."

Burnout can happen. An email I received from a memorizing friend shares her plight: "My memory work is lacking. Even recitation has become rare. Maybe you could pray for me about this. I want to delight in God's Word instead of considering memorization a chore."

Here's my response to my friend: "Do not beat yourself up. Memorizing Scripture is not the Great Commandment; it's optional. What is commanded is loving God with all your heart, soul, mind, and strength. Concentrate on loving God with all your being, and it will always lead you back to God's Word. You may need a break from memorizing, but you *never* need a break from God's Word. Take some time to go deeper in your study of a passage without memorizing it. And meditate on that passage. Remember the benefits of meditating."

Realize the spiritual warfare dimension. The enemy of your soul hates the truth and will do anything to keep you out of it. He will throw obstacles in your way, accuse you of pride or self-righteousness, and overwhelm you with the task ahead. He will attempt to discourage you and defeat you. Keep going. Keep God's Word on your lips and in your heart.

Evaluate periodically, asking yourself why you are memorizing God's Word. Keep your goal simple and focused. Walk with God and seek to please Him.

> May the words of my mouth and the meditation of my
> heart
> be pleasing in your sight,
> O Lord, my Rock and my Redeemer. (Psalm 19:14)

10 »
SMALL GROUPS

SPONTANEOUS SCRIPTURE memory groups are popping up around the country. I love it! So far, eight groups have contacted me with stories of the incredible blessings they've found in a group setting. I had a fun opportunity to Facetime with a group in Pennsylvania, encouraging them and answering their questions.

Yet many people write me saying they don't know anyone who memorizes books of the Bible and they wish they could find others. In this wonderful age of technology, we can easily connect people with each other. I invite my readers to check out our online community, (www.janetpope.org/blog/). What an incredible way to make like-minded friends and be challenged by God's Word. Let's spread the word about Scripture memory groups and see what God will do in us and through us.

WHAT DOES A SCRIPTURE
MEMORY GROUP LOOK LIKE?

Every group may be a little different, but I'll tell you about two groups: the one I'm in, and another one in West Chester, Pennsylvania.

Our group in Dallas began with three women three years ago; we now have nine. We meet on the second Monday morning of every month, in Susan's living room, from 11:00–12:00. The working women in our group meet on their lunch hour, so we keep our focus to maximize our limited time. We greet one another, open in prayer, and then take turns reciting something we've been memorizing, usually only a chapter or two.

With each recitation we draw near to God and marvel at the living words being poured over us. Nothing compares to this rich experience. Hearing the Word sparks comments and questions about the text. The reciter often shares some insight from what God is teaching her through this section of Scripture. Then we go on to the next person. Anyone is free to *pass* on the reciting part if they don't feel ready on that particular day. There's no pressure.

In our group, Lise is memorizing the book of Luke; Marty, the book of John; Tammy, the book of Joshua (seriously); Susan, the book of Galatians; Shari, Revelation 1–5; Nan just finished Psalm 34; and I'm doing 2 Corinthians. Elizabeth is in between projects, and our newest member, Rae Ann, is eager to settle on a passage and jump in. The variety of Scripture texts that we recite always confirms that every book of God's Word links together and forms one unifying theme. This sacred hour, while we hear other daughters of God speak the words of God, ignites a mini-revival in us, and we leave with spirits lifted and hearts emboldened.

The West Chester group began four years ago with four women. Now they have a core group of around fifteen members (fourteen women and one man). They meet once a month in Cathy Blair's home for one hour and fifteen minutes. During that time they tell what God is teaching them through their memory work, discuss various methods of memorizing and reviewing, share suggestions from what has helped them, and then they recite. Sometimes they recite as a group, and other times they break into groups of two or three so that each one has the opportunity to recite what they've been working on. No one is ever put on the spot to recite; it's always optional. At a recent meeting they each shared their memorization goals for the coming year.

WHAT ARE THE BENEFITS?

Among the many benefits of having a group, there are three primary ones: inspiration, accountability, and practical help.

The deep fellowship of this holy huddle inspires everyone to greater depths of knowing and loving God. Listening to God's Word energizes and invigorates. With refreshing candor we share both the desire and the struggle to live what we know. During seasons of weariness, the recitation of God's Word brings water from the well.

Accountability gives teeth to our goals. Someone might say, "Next meeting, I'm going to recite James chapter 2." This keeps them moving along with a target and a deadline. Last year, I recited a chapter or two of Esther each month, which kept me polishing it and keeping it fresh. I needed that.

A group provides a perfect place to ask for help and suggestions on verses that trip us up. Group members share technique tips like *links for kinks* and *flags for snags,* which I explained in the last chapter. We give advice from our experiences and warn of potential pitfalls in certain books. We have each other on a group email, so we can also send out a question if it can't wait until our next meeting.

HOW TO GET A GROUP STARTED

Find one or two other people committed to memorizing passages. Begin to meet regularly (weekly or monthly) for accountability and encouragement. Recite Scripture to each other. Over time ask others to join you.

One idea is to invite over a few friends who love God's Word. Recite a psalm or a book you have memorized. Tell how memorizing has affected you and ask if anyone wants to join with you in a small group.

You can also use this book as a tool for getting a group together. In the appendix, a week-by-week guide leads you through an eight-week, small-group study. This can be done in a home, church, or community center. Offer to lead others through a study of *His Word in My Heart*. When the eight-week study is over, see if anyone wants to continue meeting in a memorizing group.

After you have a consistent group, you may want to choose a name. Our group is called the BMWs (Bible Memory Women). The Pennsylvania group call themselves the Word Warriors. Another group I heard about is the M&Ms (for Memorize and Meditate). Make your name fun and meaningful.

WHAT TO DO DURING GROUP MEETINGS

With a new group, all of you may want to memorize the same thing initially (Psalm 1, and then Titus). After that, each person will be more motivated if each picks his or her own passage. Since people memorize at different rates, allow each one to go at their own pace.

Reciting and sharing will be the primary emphasis of the group. I recommend taking turns. It may feel awkward at first—in fact, it probably will—but after a few times you will see the incredible fruit that comes from being vulnerable. It doesn't matter if you have sweaty palms, or if you need to close your eyes or stare at the wall while reciting. It gets easier and more natural with time. Make reciting a priority, but not mandatory, for every person at every meeting.

Include a time of sharing how memorizing God's Word is changing you on the inside. Tell how you are applying the passage you're working on. Share insights, tips, and techniques that will help others.

Begin and end on time. This assures the members that their commitment will not be stretched. Keep focused on the purpose of the group. At the beginning of each gathering ask who will be reciting so that enough time is allocated. Whatever else you choose to do in your group is up to you.

ONLINE COMMUNITY

Our website is meant to grow a sense of community online for Scripture memorizers. We keep three areas of focus in mind.

A Resource for Memorizers

Our community is a place with loads of encouragement, practical suggestions, and tips for redeeming wasted time. You can ask questions, share insights, and learn from others. Articles, testimonials, links to helpful websites, and many other resources will equip you with tools for your success in memorizing.

To Connect People into Groups

As your group forms, we'd love to hear about it. We will register groups by location, so others can find a group near them. New start-up groups can invite others to join them.

To Provide Online Groups

Another option is to join an online group and do a book together. A long book, like Romans, would be helpful to do with others, providing accountability and encouragement.

The online community will exhort one another to hold fast to God's Word, to drink it in and live it out. Let's keep the movement going, growing joyful people passionate about God's Word and committed to memorizing chunks of it. We can turn the tide on biblical illiteracy. We can help others walk closely with God, fortify their faith, and contribute to strong and healthy churches.

> Two are better than one,
>> because they have a good return for their work:
> If one falls down,
>> his friend can help him up.
> But pity the man who falls
>> and has no one to help him up!
> Also, if two lie down together, they will keep warm.
>> But how can one keep warm alone?
> Though one may be overpowered,
>> two can defend themselves.
> A cord of three strands is not quickly broken.
> (Ecclesiastes 4:9–12)

11»
YOUR STORY: FORK IN THE ROAD

FOLLOW THE YELLOW BRICK ROAD. When Dorothy found herself in a strange place and didn't know how to get home, this pigtailed girl from Kansas heeded the advice of a dubious band of Munchkins. Dorothy and her dog, Toto, met other needy misfits along the way, locked arms, and empowered themselves with the mantra *Follow the yellow brick road.* Reaching the wizard was their mission, and this road would lead them there. Danger, discouragement, and an evil witch confronted them along the way, but they pressed on with hopes alive.

The yellow brick road ended with a bitter discovery. The Emerald City glittered, but the landlord was a fraud. Dorothy's eyes opened to the truth—she'd wasted a lot of time on that road and had led others astray as well. Why did she listen to an unreliable source and take an unproven path? Was there no other option? Ah, yes, her ruby slippers, given to her for such a purpose. She knew they were special but underestimated their usefulness.

We love this classic movie. In the end, Dorothy and her friends got what they wanted, evil was defeated, and all were reminded, "There's no place like home."

Okay, it's just a fairy tale! But can you see the parallel? That bunch of broken misfits—that's us. We wake up in a strange place trapped by our inability to help ourselves. We know we need God, every day and in every way. Yellow brick roads beckon us to follow and promise something grand, but they turn out to be a sham. So how will we find God? The only proven, time-tested road that leads to God is the Bible—that's why He gave it to us. Many grant verbal allegiance to the Bible but underestimate its usefulness. Knowing the Bible is not our ultimate aim. The goal is to know God. He alone can bind up our wounds, make sense of our lives, and equip us to live out our calling on this earth.

When we follow the *latest thing* endorsed by the masses, it may take us on an intriguing adventure. But in the end that path is a cliff with no bridge; it doesn't get us where we want to go. Yellow brick roads waste our time and lead others on a dead-end trip, all while we're feeling safety in numbers.

I became a Christian at age twenty-one. For the next fourteen years I considered myself a sincere and dedicated Christian. I loved the Lord. But I wasn't serious about His Word. I felt comfortable fitting right in with the majority. I measured myself by others and thought I was doing pretty well considering I hadn't grown up in church. I knew as much as the next guy, which in reality wasn't very much.

God brought me to a fork in the road when I was thirty-five years old. By now you know my story. After hearing God's Word spoken by a nameless woman, an unquenched thirst sent me looking for water. I began by memorizing the book of Ephesians and then went on to 2 Peter. In chapter one, I came face-to-face with these words: "His divine power has given us everything we need for life and godliness through our knowledge of Him."

I said the words over and over, thinking through the ramifications. With sheer honesty I asked myself, "Do I believe this, yes or no?" It came down to a more fundamental issue: Do I believe the Bible is true?

If I say *no*, then why give any more time to God's Word? I don't need a book of suggestions.

If I say *Yes, I do believe this*, then I'm saying much more. If I believe God's Word is absolutely true beyond question and I don't follow that up by giving my life to know and live what's in it, then I'm a fool. That's a much bigger issue!

So either I believe it or I don't. One of my biggest hesitations was that I didn't see other believers pursuing the Bible as the matrix of their lives. For most, the Bible served as a good devotional aid. But once again, although that clouded my resolve, it was *not* the issue.

I stood at the fork in the road. I waited and waited, counting the cost. Both options would alter how I lived from then on. I settled the matter that night. I moved beyond *hoping* the Bible is true to staking my life on it.

It's been my intention from the beginning to bring you to a fork in your own road. I told you my story. I showed you that memorizing passages is achievable for busy people at all stages of life. I walked you through Psalm 1 and Titus. I tried to dethrone myself as the *queen of discipline.* Testimonies from others confirmed the benefits of knowledge, sanctification, and transformed thinking. I wanted to inspire you to buy in, establish you on some new tracks, and give you enough motivation to keep going.

If you have done Psalm 1 and the book of Titus, you have tasted the sweetness. You have turned idle minutes in your day into moments shared with God. And you surprised yourself with how doable this really is.

So where do you go from here? Do you see yourself

standing at a fork in the road? Which fork should you take? As in any road trip, everything depends on *where you want to end up*.

Think long-term for a minute. Twenty years will come and go. How would you hope to describe yourself and your walk with God in twenty years? Which road will take you there?

Do you want to be a godly, wise person who knows the heart of God and lives in light of His Word? You will not become this person by default. You will only become what you are in the process of becoming. It requires deliberate choices to get to know God's Word and meditate on it daily, thoroughly, intentionally. You will find the highway to a closer walk with God paved with Scripture. Everything else is a yellow brick road, a costly diversion that will keep you from things that matter most.

Evaluate your current method of learning and applying God's Word. What is your specific plan, and how's it working for you? Memorizing passages is not the only way to arrive at the goal. But if the path you've been on for the past few years has not reaped those benefits, then you should change roads. I've shown you an alternative, one option.

How will I present my closing charge to you? Based upon a multitude of emails, I know that different personality types react differently.

Some of you respond well to a robust challenge. Your adventurous side dares the summit, ventures out at great risk, and takes the gravel path over the paved road. You love to be prodded and pushed beyond yourself for the payoff at journey's end.

To all of you I say, leave the security of your routine.

Abandon the ditch you've made by your old habits. Chase after the God who chased after you, and don't stop till you've embraced Him in all His magnificence. Arm yourself with Scripture, and train yourself to be a godly warrior. Battle the enticements of this age with the sword of truth, and fight the enemy within who tempts you to be a slacker. Don't take shortcuts. Forge ahead on the narrow alley with God's Word lighting the way. Don't look back. Say no to all yellow brick roads.

Some of you, however, do not respond well to an aggressive challenge. Instead, you recoil at ultimatums. Too much pressure puts the squeeze on you. Skepticism or fear of failure immobilizes you, and your self-protection mode takes over.

My ping-pong personality plays both sides. Too many times I take the bait on a challenge, but then the quitter in me raises her ugly head and down we go. Looking in the mirror with disappointment in myself takes me lower than when I started. It's too risky, my self-esteem too fragile. You may recall what fueled my motivation early on: I couldn't handle the devastation of another goal abandoned.

A few weeks ago I spoke in a local women's prison. I recited the passage known as the Upper Room Discourse, John 13–17. A woman volunteer from a local church, obviously moved by God's Word spoken, told me she had never heard anything like it and was mesmerized. I totally get that—that was *me* twenty years ago in Chattanooga. I gave her a copy of my book and invited her to our Scripture memory group. She emailed me, saying, "I am encouraged and inspired, yet afraid all at the same time. I have never considered memorizing the Word as you have, however I am intrigued. My immediate concern (fear): Would I be faithful?"

My heart dropped as I read the familiar response. Her doubt was *not* in the power of God's Word to do something amazing in her life. Her doubt was in *herself*. Many identify with her hesitation. But eyes-on-self is a yellow brick road; it will not take you where you want to end up. One of the reasons I continue to memorize is to get my eyes *off* myself and onto God. I've already tried the self-absorbed life and found it an endless toll road.

To you who don't want a rousing challenge, I understand. To you I say, Don't think of memorizing passages as something *to do* but rather Someone worthy to pursue.

Pursue the One who spoke a million galaxies into space and whose word holds them in perfect tension. The One enthroned above the cherubim, who dwells in unapproachable light—He is worthy.

Pursue the One who set aside His majesty to take on human skin. The One who wooed you, called your name, and paid your ransom—He is worthy.

Pursue the One who breathes life into paper and ink to reveal His ways to hungry seekers. The One who binds Himself to His Word till every promise comes to pass—He is worthy.

Make God your heart's fullest joy, and no worldly pleasure will be able to compete.

If you've found a better way to walk closely with God, then stay with it. If not, I offer you another option.

Take baby steps if you're cautious. Take giant steps if you dare. Either way, take hold of God's Word and let God's Word take hold of you.

Janet Pope's speaking ministry
includes women's conferences,
retreats, and other gatherings.
Contact her at janet@janetpope.org.

WEEKLY SMALL GROUP STUDY QUESTIONS

Week	Homework	Group Interaction Questions

1	none	Distribute books.
		Each person share:
		  introductions
		  expectations for the study
		  any previous experience memorizing passages
		One person read the introduction from *His Word in My Heart* (4½ minutes).
		Overview homework for all 8 weeks.

2	Read chapters 1–3. Memorize & meditate on Psalm 1.	What should be the goal of memorizing Scripture? Why does God call the man in Psalm 1 blessed? What have you seen to be the benefits so far? When have you found time during your day? What questions do you have about memorizing? What tips can you offer to others? Take turns reciting Psalm 1 (optional).
3	Read chapters 4–5. Memorize & meditate on Titus 1:1–7.	What are some of the implications of 2 Peter 1:3? What is the relationship between knowledge and a close relationship with God? How did God plan for His children to get to know Him? What are some benefits of memorizing passages instead of selected verses? How does trusting God relate to our knowledge of God? What are some things you learned in the verses you memorized this week? Ask any questions you have about memorizing. Share tips. Take turns reciting either Psalm 1 or Titus 1:1–7 (optional).

Week	Homework	Group Interaction Questions
4	Read chapter 6. Memorize & meditate on Titus 1:8–14.	How does God use His Word to bring about our sanctification? Can you see areas in your life that need to align with God's Word? Where does obedience to God's Word fit into sanctification? How does God's Word help us obey? What are some things you learned in the verses you memorized this week? Ask any questions you have about memorizing. Share tips. Take turns reciting Psalm 1 or any portion of Titus 1 (optional).
5	Read chapter 7. Memorize and meditate on Titus 1:15–16. Memorize and meditate on Titus 2:1–5.	Discuss the relationship between desire and discipline. How does memorizing Scripture help with desire and discipline? What benefit have you found in meditating on the Scripture you memorize? What are some benefits of memorizing Titus vs. reading it? What are some things you learned in the verses you memorized this week? Ask any questions you have about memorizing. Share tips. Take turns reciting Psalm 1 or portions of Titus (optional).
6	Read chapter 8. Memorize and meditate on Titus 2:6–12.	How does learning a language parallel transformed thinking? Why do we need transformed thinking? (Four reasons) What does transformed thinking look like? How do we get transformed thinking? How does memorizing Scripture help? What are some things you learned in the verses you memorized this week? Ask any questions you have about memorizing. Share tips. Take turns reciting Psalm 1 or portions of Titus (optional).

Week	Homework	Group Interaction Questions
7	Read chapters 9–10. Memorize and meditate on Titus 2:13–15. Memorize and meditate on Titus 3:1–5.	What are some of the benefits of reviewing what you have memorized? Discuss the usefulness of using different methods of review. Have you developed a system that works for you? Which technologies are you using to memorize? Which tips in chapter 9 did you find helpful? What benefits have you experienced from a group setting? Would you benefit from continuing in a Scripture memory group? What are some things you learned in the verses you memorized this week? Ask any questions you have about memorizing. Share tips. Take turns reciting Psalm 1 or portions of Titus (optional).
8	Read chapter 11. Memorize and meditate on Titus 3:6–12.	What is the benefit of a metaphorical fork in the road? Do you see yourself at a fork in your road? Where would you like to be in twenty years in terms of your relationship with God? What is your plan to make that a reality? Make a distinction between Scripture memory as something to do vs. Someone to pursue. What are some things you learned in the verses you memorized this week? Ask any questions you have about memorizing. Share tips. Take turns reciting Psalm 1 or portions of Titus (optional). Close the study with a prayer that all would become like the blessed man in Psalm 1.

ACKNOWLEDGMENTS

BMWs (the Bible Memory Women): Our lips speak forth the Word of God, and our hearts marvel at the Author; the joy spills over!

Left2write (writers' group): You nurture my nouns, vibrate my verbs, and polish my pearls.

Richie Malone & the Bible Girls: Seven years of mountain retreats, a refuge from the chaos, and pinnacle moments that linger till next year.

Ministry partners: Your prayers and financial support contribute to my life and ministry beyond measure.

NOTES

Chapter 2 • My Goals: Then & Now

1. Spiros Zodhiates, *The Complete Word Study: Old Testament,* gen. ed., Warren Baker (Chattanooga, TN: AMG, 1994), entry no. 1897, 2310.

Chapter 7 • Your Turn: Soak It In

2. A. W. Tozer, *The Pursuit of God* (Camp Hill, PA: Christian Publications, Inc., 1982), 20.

Chapter 8 • The Benefits of Transformed Thinking

3. Cleon L. Rogers Jr. and Cleon L. Rogers III, *The New Linguistic and Exegetical Key to the Greek New Testament* (Grand Rapids: Zondervan, 1998), 339.

THE QUIET PLACE

Bestselling author Nancy Leigh DeMoss adapts the core themes of her teaching into a format her fans can enjoy daily-366 portions of rich Bible study and practical applications.

Also available as an ebook

www.MoodyPublishers.com